TURN IN YOUR
CAPTIVITY

TURN IN YOUR CAPTIVITY

Ending Abuse in Marriages & Relationships The Jesus Way

SANDRA WILSON

Tate Publishing & *Enterprises*

Turn In Your Captivity!
Copyright © 2007 by Sandra Wilson. All rights reserved.

This title is also available as a Tate Out Loud product. Visit www.tatepublishing.com for more information.

No part of this publication may be reproduced, stored in a retrieval system or transmitted in any way by any means, electronic, mechanical, photocopy, recording or otherwise without the prior permission of the author except as provided by USA copyright law.

Scripture quotations are taken from the *Holy Bible, King James Version*, Cambridge, 1769. Used by permission. All rights reserved

Scripture quotations marked "NLT" are taken from the *Holy Bible, New Living Translation*, Copyright © 1996. Used by permission of Tyndale House Publishers, Inc. All rights reserved.

The opinions expressed by the author are not necessarily those of Tate Publishing, LLC.This book is designed to provide accurate and authoritative information with regard to the subject matter covered. This information is given with the understanding that neither the author nor Tate Publishing, LLC is engaged in rendering legal, professional advice. Since the details of your situation are fact dependent, you should additionally seek the services of a competent professional.

The opinions expressed by the author are not necessarily those of Tate Publishing, LLC.

Published by Tate Publishing & Enterprises, LLC
127 E. Trade Center Terrace | Mustang, Oklahoma 73064 USA
1.888.361.9473 | www.tatepublishing.com

Tate Publishing is committed to excellence in the publishing industry. The company reflects the philosophy established by the founders, based on Psalms 68:11,
"*The Lord gave the word and great was the company of those who published it.*"

Book design copyright © 2007 by Tate Publishing, LLC. All rights reserved.
Cover design by Lindsay B. Behrens
Interior design by Kellie Southerland

Published in the United States of America

ISBN: 9781-6024700-0-2
1. Adult Nonfiction   2. Poetry
3. Christian Life   4. Marriage and Divorce
07.07.17

To the soundness and perfecting skills imparted
to those who walk in The Jesus Way.

To my mother, Annie Bell Washington;
grandmother, Callie Washington; and aunt Betty Faulkner,
for their help through revelation knowledge.

And he (God) said unto me, Write: for these words are true and faithful. Revelation 21:5

…Write thee all the words that I have spoken unto thee in a book. Jeremiah 30:2

Acknowledgments

Where there is rhyme; there is a reason,
the gift of rhyme to use in all of my seasons.
For Jesus Christ is the rhythm of the time
to use my anointed gift of rhyme.

This assignment could not have been envisioned nor accomplished without assistance from the Trinity: the Father, the Son, and the Holy Ghost; and the Name of Jesus, the Blood of Jesus, and God's Mighty Hammer…His Word.

To my family for their love and support during my season from mourning to Morning Glory: father, Albert Washington; step mother, Alta Washington; sisters: Barbara Washington, Doris Taylor, Brenda Washington, Pamela Meriwether, and Starlet Washington; brother, Melvin Washington; nieces, nephews; and Mississippi/Illinois family of uncles, aunts and cousins, you know who you are!

To my Pastors, Drs. Leo and Alma Holt and the Grace Christian Fellowship Church International family in Memphis, Tennessee, a Supernatural church, that helped me develop the skill to become a Superordinary person doing Supernatural things for a Supernatural God.

To my twin sister in the Lord and ministry partner, Prophetess Angela Jenkins Newton, for the strength, spiritual maturity, friendship, and joy that she imparts to my life.

And to my friends for their blessings of encouragement, prayers, lunch dates, and shopping trips: Tina White, Gloria Myers, Deborah Mitchell, Beulah Mitchell, Cynthia Johnson, Rita Briggs, Sarah Stokes, Teresa Green, Bridgett Watson, LaTonya Hudson, Alberta Bell, Judith Levy, Billy and Mary Coleman, Ann Hurt, Judith Pleas, Sarah Gordon, and Ruth Becks.

Table of Contents

Turn In Your Captivity! 17
The Jesus Way 19
Introduction. 21

Chapter 1. Torment, Fear, Abandonment, And Oppressive Abuse (Evil Against The Jesus Way!). 25
    Morning Glory. 28
    Free From The Law Story 31
    Personal Bill Of Rights 35
    Husband, Do You Love Me? 37
    Adultery Story 40
    Obesity Story. 44
    Will He Marry Me? 47
    Domestic Violence Story 49
    Wicked People 53
    Worship The Lord God Only 56
    Witchcraft, Sorcery In Our Society 61

Stand In The Gap 66
Mental and Emotional Oppression Story 69
All Have Sinned Versus Wickedness .74
Yield Not To Temptation. 80
Responsible Forgiveness. 83
Why Do You Watch Over Me Lord? 86
I Hit Him! 89
Abandonment Story. 92
Could It Be?. 95
A Sister's Love 98
The Avenging Angel 100
The Van Back! 102
Look-Out For Love. 105
At First. 107
Increasing Their Own Kill. 110
God Is Not In Your Past, So Why Are You? 114
In Righteousness Shall You Be Established. 117
To Those Who Are Wicked 120
I Knew Pain 123
Suicide Prevention 126
Lemonade Or Gatorade? 129
"Women Take Care Of Your Temple" 131
Stop Sacrificing Yourself, Yourself .134

Chapter 2. Jesus Loves and Cares For Us
(He's Just That Way!) 137
This Is The Man 140
A Man Named Jesus Christ. 145
God's Captivity Training 149

Good Watchman Story 156
Who Knows…But Jesus? 159
With Empathy 161
Rather Than The Other 163
Your Self-Worth 166
Today Is The Day 170
Goodness! 173
Praise The Lord! 174
The Prayer 176

Chapter 3. Overcoming Oppressive Captivity (Using The Jesus Way CRNPF!) .181
Turn and Surrender 187
The Jesus Way 189
Negotiation Story 191
O God Of Vengeance 197
Avenging Story 199
Did You Know? 201
Pursuit Of Love 203
The Confrontation Story 206
Spiritual Protection 209
Separation Time Story 212
The Shelter Of The Most High .218
Fear Buster! 220
The Jesus Way Training School 223
Spiritual Warfare 229
Come Out From The Inside! 232
When Going Through 236
The Lifter Of My Head 239

Death and Confusion..241
"The Little Engine That Could"......................243
How Not To Be Hurt Again 246
He Has Made Me Glad!................................250
He Thought...253
"Thought Victor" Not "Victim"......................256
"Tongue Victor" Not "Victim"........................259
"Action Victor" Not "Victim"..........................262
"The Wait"..264
"A Time" 266
Turn In Our Captivity 268
Stand In Your Fight The Key Is To Fight 270
Hold and Rock Me Jesus!..............................275
The Call..278
A Feather On The Couch 280
God's Mighty Hammer!..............................282
Again, God's Mighty Hammer!......................284
Like Bees 287
The Growl...289
The Repo Man..291

Chapter 4. Living in Victory (The Jesus Way!)............295
Whoever Is Victorious.................................297
You Thrill Me Lord! 299
What A Wonderful Time!............................301
My Man...303
On The Wings Of Love 305
Reminds Me Of Our Love 307
2 (Two)...309

Your Smile 311
Sweet Music Together 313
Forgive Me. 315
Still A Sister Of Mine 317
Brother. 319
Daddy. 321
"Mama, Thank You". 323
My Mama's Dedication 325
My Family Love Memories 327

Bibliography 336

Turn In Your Captivity!

Turn again our captivity, O LORD, as the streams in the south. They that sow in tears shall reap joy. He that goeth forth and weepeth, bearing precious seeds, shall doubtless come again with rejoicing, bringing his sheaves *with him* (Psalm 126:4–6).

All along your journey in The Jesus Way you will pick up speed and skill needed to make the "whole turn," operating in the *whole counsel* of God. Many of you shall go forth out of the city, and shall dwell in the field. There you shall be delivered. And there the Lord shall redeem you from the hands of your enemies (Micah 4:10). "Sowing" is a quarter of the turn; "Going Forth" is half of the turn; "Bearing" is three quarters of the turn; but praise God! "Coming Again" is the *wholeness* of the turn. And you will be "Bringing" your reaping full speed upon the heads of Satan and his kingdom, like the Ram of God that you have *turned* to be!

WHEN the LORD turned again the captivity...we were like them that dream. Then was our mouth filled with laughter, and our tongue with singing: then said they...The LORD hath done great things for them (Psalm 126:1–2).

The Jesus Way

*Jesus saith unto him, I am the way, the truth, and the life:
no man cometh unto the Father, but by me.*
John 14:6

The Jesus Way represents whether each of us will say "Yes" to the robe of righteousness being continually extended; and "Yes" to taking up our cross and following after Jesus. Jesus suffered tremendously to make the robe of righteousness available to us. It is a *required* drape from the Lord, a protective covering to keep our clothing of salvation white; thereby, maintaining right standing and fellowship with God. As the prophet Isaiah, will you say, *"I am overwhelmed with joy in the Lord my God! For He has dressed me with the clothing of salvation and draped me in a robe of righteousness* (Isaiah 61:10, NLT)?" Will you take up your cross and follow after Jesus? He is not an evil taskmaster! He will put no more on us than we can bear. Jesus makes His yoke easy and His burdens light. He is our example to not oppress, afflict and grieve others through unjust treatment.

We should adamantly renounce the robe that Satan continuously tries to force us to wear. His robe is a robe of heaviness, a filthy garment with holes, which do not cover our shame. It displays all the stains from our unrepentant sins and life's wounds. Jesus does not want to see us marred; nor our nakedness, and others laughing and pointing at our shame! Our nakedness has brought about our fears, and our fears have caused us to hide ourselves and choose not to move boldly *to* and *in* our God-appointed destiny.

But the Good News is that we can pull off every weight and sin which so easily beset us and run with patience to the God ordained finish line of our destiny. Let us therefore cast off the works of darkness, and let us put on the armor of light. Let us put on the Lord Jesus Christ, and make no provision to fulfill the lusts of the flesh. It is a wise exchange, because for the captivity that we shed, The Jesus Way will give us a tender heart for our heart of stone…beauty for our ashes…oil of joy for our mourning…and garment of praise for our spirit of heaviness (Isaiah 61:3).

Introduction

Turn In Your Captivity, Ending Abuse in Marriages and Relationships The Jesus Way addresses a serious and growing problem in our society today...Intimate Partner Violence (IPV), marital and relational abuse. IPV is a significant threat to the health and well-being of the individual who finds him or herself captive in this type of abuse. Statistics show that approximately 28% of abuse against women was at the hand of their intimate partner such as a husband or boyfriend. In contrast, victimization of men by their intimate partner accounted for only 5%. Men were significantly more likely to have been victimized by acquaintances (50%) or strangers (44%) than by their intimate partners. Each year, thousands of women, about one in three, are physically, emotionally, sexually, and verbally abused. The Wellesley Centers for Women report that there is some evidence that African-American women may be at an increased risk. It is estimated that African-American women experience IPV at a rate 35% higher than that of White women. The leading cause of death among African-American women ages 15–45 is homicide at the hands of a male intimate partner. But not only are African-American women experiencing Intimate Partner Violence, the truth is IPV is a common pervasive problem that transcends culture, ethnicity, and economic status.

Jesus is a Wonderful Counselor and His example provides us with concrete answers to all of life's problems. His death and resurrection made us free from every form of oppression, reinstated our power and authority over Satanic influences, and showed us the way to victorious living. These anointed poems and poetic stories are a teaching tool for those who find themselves under the afflictions of their own captive sins: (i.e. perfectionism, depression, low self-esteem, sexual immorality, eating disorders, etc.); as well as victims at the hand of abusive individuals who wound, sadden, control, abandon, deceive, inflict mental, physical and spiritual oppression, and even murder. They provide Jesus' instructions on how to develop godly skills and integrity in dealing with ourselves and wicked individuals. There are those who lack teaching and therefore remain in captivity and become abusers due to ignorance and error. Then there are those who know what is right, but deliberately and persistently rebel and delight in causing grievous afflictions to others. Through The Jesus Way, we learn the skill to put on the whole armor of God to fight against witchcraft, sorcery, gangster and mafia spirits, fear; as well as demonic, evil and unclean spirits that are formed against us. This will surely bring a drastic move of God and a swift healing to marriages and relationships.

Turn In Your Captivity, Ending Abuse in Marriages and Relationships The Jesus Way ministers to men as well as women. It is foremost written to help women who lack godly skills, as well as those who are grieving as a result of spousal abandonment, mental, emotional, spiritual, and physically abusive relationships. But it also addresses those same issues for men. Men can be held captive and battered at the hand of an abusive woman as well. They too need assistance achieving victory within the same crisis. The purpose of these writings is to empower oppressed men and women, and to let them know that God sees the abuse and hears their cries. Its goal is to teach victims of abuse how to cease being an abuser of themselves; as well as opening the eyes of abusers to discern that they too are in captivity, teaching both parties how to break from the influences of Satan. Jesus said, *Come to me, all of you who are weary and carry heavy burdens, and I will give you rest* (Matthew 11:28, NLT). Deep counsel and understanding is His because His thoughts are very deep and He speaks directly to our hearts.

Given that many in captivity want the abuse to end, but not the relationship, what alternatives are there for stopping the abuse? What can be done to help the abuser change his or her ways and to protect the victim and others in the meantime? The Jesus Way CRNPF (**C**onfront, **R**ebuke, **N**egotiate, **P**rayer, and **F**aith), as discussed in chapter three, are deep teachings of God for the building of skills needed for spiritual warfare in marriages and relationships. These are all ordained strategies of God and ones that Jesus also used. All throughout the bible Jesus ordained and endorsed these Faith fighting techniques: *the Word, tithes and offerings, praise and worship, prayer, fasting, anointed oil, breaking of bread, and testimonials.*

The Jesus Way (CRNPF) helped me to gain victory from my oppressive captivity; for I felt I would never be strong enough to face this issue. I suffered captivity for 20 years in two marriages due to my lack of godly skills and inflictions of marital abuse and abandonment placed by others. The Jesus Way equipped me with the skill of obedience to surrender to God and release toxic individuals from my life. God says, *Now is the time for those in captivity to be no longer ignorant of My ways. I will teach them, through my Son, Jesus, how to come out of captivity and establish the peace within marriages and relationships as I intended. But for some, it will be the season of separation, because of being joined to an anti-christ spirit.*

Those making the *turn in their captivity* have the promise of God's protection and rewards, providing power to sustain them to the end… an end that carries their hopes and expectations. Whereas for those who *refuse to turn themselves*, God promises punishment and avenge upon their heads on behalf of those they oppress. Witnessing the light and abundant life of The Jesus Way, abusers will have enough shame, fear and conviction to make the *turn in their captivity* as well.

Receive The Jesus Way into your heart and allow Him to remove your hurts and pain. Enjoy being transformed from mourning to Morning Glory, for the battle belongs to God. Stand still and see the awesomeness of God work on your behalf. The Jesus Way will stand beside you as you shout praises unto our Wonderful Counselor, who has caused the *Turn In Your Captivity!*

Chapter 1
Captive Torment, Control, Fear, Abandonment and Oppressive Abuse
(Evil Against The Jesus Way!)

Mankind was created in the image of God and received an honored work assignment and blessed covenant. Satan wants to spoil that image, distract us from our work assignment, and steal our blessings. He does this by deceiving us into worshipping him, and not God. Satan's pride caused him to lose his position in heaven as a mighty angelic being. His jealousy of God led to his downfall. He allowed his wealth, beauty and splendor to change him from blameless to one who possessed many sins: violence, pride, corrupt wisdom and dishonest trade (Ezekiel 28:12–19). He is angry and vengeful because God expelled him and his angels from heaven. And even as an outcast on earth, he is still jealous of God. That is why he uses mankind in his games against God, while being an opposing copy cat. In fact, his interest is only to steal, kill and destroy us. Satan thought deceiving Adam and Eve in the garden of Eden sealed mankind's fate; but Jesus Christ restored us to the righteousness of God! Satan wants what we have in Christ Jesus, and is envious that he cannot be restored to his former glory. The bible says Satan and his kingdom daily try to crucify Jesus anew and put Him to an opened shame (Hebrews 6:6).

We can become enemies of God by allowing ourselves to be influenced by Satan to where we inflict pain and bondage onto ourselves and extend it to others, causing their captivity as well. Satan and his army know that they are already defeated and have lost the spiritual war against God, but they are fighting hard to try to get victory over *our* individual battles, lives, and souls. From the days of John the Baptist until now, the kingdom of heaven suffer violence, and the violent take it by force (Matthew 11:12). Satan can influence others, especially our dearest loved ones, to inflict such grief and oppression upon us to where we can become overwhelmed, broken, sad, fearful, and suicidal.

We have to become wise to the strategies Satan uses and gives to those under his influence. According to the Wellesley Center for Women, an abuser uses strategies of pretense, social isolation, control, and threats. Initially an abuser can come across as charming and romantic, and uses positive interpersonal behaviors to attract his victim. He or she can be quite charming to those outside of the home as well. It might not be until well into the relationship, after some form of commitment has been made, when the abuse starts. Even if the abuse begins much earlier, it often starts with "minor" acts and can be easily dismissed. The abuser appears to be remorseful, skilled at the pretense of innocence, and is quite adept at deflecting blame onto the victim. This traps the victim in a cycle in which he or she keeps trying to avoid abuse by satisfying, and even anticipating, the abuser's every whim and mood. The victim fails, of course, because only the abuser is responsible for his or her behavior. The goals of social isolation and control are designed to weaken or remove the social supports upon which the partner can rely, making it more difficult for him or her to escape or to get help. Much of the abuser's time and energy is spent on surveillance, limiting comings and goings, monitoring internet activity and telephone calls. They actively try to interfere with relationships with family and friends and discourage the formation of new friendships. Abusers tend to limit their partner's access to money by preventing them from working or interfers with their employment so that they lose their jobs. Threats and fear tactics are used in an effort to coerce their partner not to leave or to come back. Greater harm is threatened and can extend to the children, family members, friends, or anyone who tries to help. Other threats can come in the form of a kidnap or denied access to the children, or harming or killing a companion's pet.

For many marriages and relationships today, there is no godly order in place; therefore, a grieving spirit becomes the norm. One individual is dealing treacherously, while the other works to maintain their relationship or marriage. We have to protect our spirit. God has set our spirit to bear witness of us in the earth (I John 5:8). Our spirit should not be grieved; but excellent and faithful (Proverbs 11:13; 17:27). If our spirit remains grieved and we become content with captivity, what kind of an example of light are we? A spirit that is anguished is sometimes unable to heed the voice of God, because terror causes distraction. This can result in one captivity multiplying into many others.

Jesus said, *Behold, I send you forth as sheep in the midst of wolves: be ye therefore wise as serpents but harmless as doves* (Matthew 10:16). We all are among wolves; in one form or fashion…even in our own homes. God not only warns us about wolves, but against false prophets (who are wolves in sheep's clothing), hirelings (who are in the relationship just for what they can get), strangers (who try to sway you to idol doctrines), foxes, dogs, bulls, lions, serpents, scorpions, briers and thorns. But the Good News is that through the blood of Christ Jesus, we have power against evil principalities…against rulers of the darkness of this world…and against spiritual wickedness in high places (Ephesians 6:12).

Welcome to the deep teachings on how to *End Abuse in Marriages and Relationships The Jesus Way* using God's growth process and Jesus' right response to complicated, emotionally charged, and often times, dangerous situations. If you are a victim of abuse and/or an abuser, the hope is that by the understanding of God's standards and promises to those who walk The Jesus Way, and His vengeance upon those who inflict abuse, you will be launched into making the whole *Turn In Your Captivity*.

Morning Glory

If my life resembles a garbage dump,
it's up to me to sort it through,
turn over soil…plant flowers.

Today, I start the process of being gentle to myself,
minute by minute…hour by hour.

As I unwrap myself, I ask that you be patient and kind;
for I'm just a morning glory, lost in a tangle of vines.

If I do too much out of fear and self-abuse,
it's up to me to become honest with myself,
overcoming my addictions.

Today, I start the process of being aware
of all of my own self-imposed afflictions.

As I unwrap myself, I ask that you be patient and kind;
for I'm just a morning glory, lost in a tangle of vines.

If I believe others deem me as indispensable,
convinced this perception holds true,
it's my control illusion
I need to force myself to see.

Today, I start the process of asking,
"Am I expendable to me?"
Now that's the question!
That's the question that be!

*As I unwrap myself, I ask that you be patient and kind;
for I'm just a morning glory, lost in a tangle of vines.*

If I'm frantic over almost anything,
it's up to me to put a stop
to where this old familiar friend abide.

Today, I start the process of evicting frantic and panic
from where they've been allowed to reside.

*As I unwrap myself, I ask that you be patient and kind;
for I'm just a morning glory, lost in a tangle of vines.*

If I'm beating myself over past mistakes,
it's up to me to stop self-harm,
self-neglect, and make self-amend.

Today, I start the process of taking stock,
moving on, becoming a self-friend.

*As I unwrap myself, I ask that you be patient and kind;
for I'm just a morning glory, lost in a tangle of vines.*

If I've swallowed beliefs from outside,
failing to go within my own awareness of God,
it's up to me to start trusting my own knowing.

Today, I start the process of being
spiritually connected with who I am,
sprouting roots, reaching high,
and with God's light…growing.

*As I unwrap myself, I ask that you be patient and kind;
for I'm just a morning glory, lost in a tangle of vines.*

The LORD will perfect *that which* concerneth me: Psalm 138:8

Stand fast therefore in the liberty wherewith Christ hath made us free, and be not entangled again with the yoke of bondage. Galatians 5:1

ARISE, shine; for thy light is come, and the glory of the LORD is risen upon thee…and his glory shall be seen upon thee. Isaiah 60:1–2

Free From The Law Story

She hurries to answer the phone on the second ring.
The voice on the other end exclaims,
"Oh you're back!"

"Yeah, I just got back a few minutes ago.
I was taking the groceries out the sack."

"Why didn't you call me before you went,
and after you've returned home?"

"Honey, you're at work.
I just went to the store.
It's not like for hours I've been gone."

"Look, you're to call before
and after you go anywhere.
I'm not going to tolerate any more mistakes.

If you're going to be my wife,
you will follow the rules.
Mistakes you're not allowed to make."

The conversation ends.
She hangs up the phone,
and finishes putting the groceries away.

She picks up the Book,
sitting down to read.
This is what the bible had to say:

In the old way,
by obeying the written letter of the law
is how we related to God.
We tried to be obedient, but made mistakes.
Keeping every letter was hard.

God's law was not sinful,
but it showed up our sins.
We tried to be obedient with all our might.
The law gave the death penalty,
(for the wages of sin is death).
So God gave another avenue to make things right.

If there were no law,
sin would not have power. To avoid breaking the law
is to have no law to break.
For Jesus loved us so,
until He volunteered to go,
and be that avenue for mankind's sake.

God gave us a second chance
through our intercessory man,
to reestablish a relationship with Him as friends.
It's not through our works,
nor the good we've done,
but on Jesus Christ we faithfully depend.

On the cross, Jesus defeated sin and death.
It was His body and blood that paid the price.
When we became Christians and were baptized,
we died and were buried with Christ.

Christ arose from the dead and will never die again.
We're released from the captive powers
of the law and sin.

Through Christ Jesus, faith is the key.
Through God's mercy and grace,
from the law we're made free.

She closes the Book,
releasing a slow, healing sigh,
thanking God for directing her life.

She asks God to continue
to instill within her the truth,
and godly skills needed in being a wife.

"My husband needs to read this,
then maybe he can eventually see.

Because of oppressive rules, I'm overwhelmed;
I need to be made free.

Through love and respect,
mutual submission in check,
is The Jesus Way for the godly head.

And just as Jesus Christ,
My husband needs to sacrifice,
directing our marriage as Jesus has led."

There is no man that hath power over the spirit to retain the spirit: Ecclesiastes 8:8

For the law of the Spirit of life in Christ Jesus hath made me free from the law of sin and death. Romans 8:2

And that we may be delivered from unreasonable and wicked men: for all men have not faith. II Thessalonians 3:2

...their course is evil and their force *is* not right. Jeremiah 23:10

...who subvert whole houses, teaching things which they ought not...Titus 1:11

The Lord shall preserve thy going out and thy coming in from this time forth, and even for evermore. Psalm 121:8

I *am* the Lord thy God, which have brought thee out of the...house of bondage. Exodus 20:1

Personal Bill Of Rights

I have the right to be myself.

I have the right to refuse request without feeling selfish.

I have the right to feel and express anger
(but assertively—-not aggressively).

I have the right to change my mind.

I have the right to say I do not know.

I have the right to not agree.

I have the right to say I do not understand.

I have the right to ask for what I want.

I have the right to say "no" to requests.

I have the right to express my feelings
(but assertively—-not aggressively).

I have the right to make mistakes.

I have the right to not give reasons or excuses
for my behavior.

I have the right to make my own decisions.

I have the right to be in a non-abusive environment.

I have the right to have my needs and wants respected by others.

I have the right to be happy.

I have the right to be treated with dignity and respect.

For thou (Lord) hast maintained my right and my cause; thou satest in the throne judging right. Psalm 9:4

…renew a right spirit within me. Psalm 51:10

Husband, Do You Love Me?

"Husband, son of man, do you love me?"
"Yes, Lord," Husband replied, "You know I love you."
"Then feed my lamb." Jesus told him.

Jesus repeated the question:
"Husband, son of man, do you love me?"
"Yes, Lord," Husband said, "You know I love you."
"Then take care of my sheep," Jesus said.

Once more He asked him,
"Husband, son of man, do you love me?"
Husband was grieved that Jesus asked
the question a third time.
He said, "Lord, you know everything.
You know I love you."
Jesus said, "Then feed my sheep."

"I didn't give you something so precious to Me
to control, oppress and abuse.
I didn't give you something so valuable to Me
to make cry and misuse.

For you both are my workers,
but given different responsibility measures.
I assigned you as head
in accordance to God's will and pleasure.

You may feel greater,
but you're saved not by works,
lest any man should boast.

For by Grace you're saved through faith;
My sufficient Grace is what's the most.

For shepherd…and sheep,
the care they both receive
is the equality I give.
No respecter of persons,
no favorites
is how I ordained you both to live.

God put the marriage body together
where husband and wife can dwell peaceably.
Nourishing and cherishing are given to the sheep,
causing harmony and care equally.

For husband and wife are one body;
two have become one flesh.
For this cause I joined you to your wife,
commanding you to leave all the rest.

Your power through ceremonial rules
do not help those who follow them.
It causes guilt, condemnation,
and people pleasing at *your* whim.

Do I want you controlling My sheep by traditions
and man-made rules you heard?
You are ordained as a Watcher,
not a controller;
…just feed her God's Word."

His (Satan's) watchmen *are* blind: they are all ignorant, they *are* all dumb dogs, they cannot bark; sleeping, lying down, loving to slumber. Yea, *they are* greedy dogs *which* can never have enough, and they are shepherds that cannot understand: they all look to their own way, every one for his gain…Isaiah 56:10–11

…justice standeth afar off: for truth is fallen in the street, and equality cannot enter. Isaiah 59:14

…*what will he do unto those husbandmen?*…He will miserably destroy those wicked men, and will let out *his* vineyard unto other husbandmen; Matthew 21:40–41

…rules may seem wise because they require strong devotion, humility, and severe bodily discipline. But they have no effect…Colossians 2:23, NLT

…(the oppressed) they hearkened not…for anguish of spirit, and for cruel bondage. Exodus 6:9

I *am* afflicted…*while* I suffer thy terrors I am distracted. Psalm 88:15

I (Jesus) am the one who corrects and disciplines everyone I love. Revelation 3:19, NLT

The blessing of the LORD, it maketh rich, and he addeth no sorrow with it. Proverbs 10:22

Adultery Story

Is he creeping out the back door,
hoping not to be seen?
Telling the Other One he loves her,
but to the Married One he's mean.

He has stopped holding the Married One,
ceased wiping away her tears.
Instead he has replaced his loving arms
with torment and fears.

Fear that something is dreadfully wrong.
He does not act the same.
Is it just a phase he's going through,
or is it me, he's ashamed?

"I know I've gained some pounds over the years.
I know my hair is not long.
But have I been such a bad wife,
I'm causing him to do wrong?"

He tells the Other One, "I love you.
I will try to see you on tonight."
He tells the Married One
he's mad about the food,
intentionally starting the fight.

The fight that will allow him to leave the house,
and meet the Other One as planned.
The fight that will allow him to break the bond,
and pull the ring off his married hand.

Fearful he will not come home.
Convinced he was right.
Ashamed he felt the food was not good.
Mad and sad because of the fight.

"I know I'm not the best of cooks,
but he never complained before.
I must write down a list of things
to get tomorrow from the store.

I'm going to make this up to him,
the best dinner I will prepare.
This will be the best meal ever,
my darling dear, I swear."

He phones the Other One
to make plans for another date.
He phones the Married One
to lie of having to work late.

He tells the Married One not to wait,
it's going to be a long time.
The Married One bows and shakes,
staring at her table set with wine.

Fearful her fears
are coming to pass.
Fearful her marriage might not last.

Sad she's been placed
in this painful situation.
Sadness turns to anger
as she contemplates castration.

Ashamed of the thoughts
entering her mind.
She knows this will lead
to her doing jail time.

She goes down on her knees
to talk to her One and Only saving grace.
With Jesus Christ is where she wants to be
more than any other place.

This man, Jesus, provides her
with comfort in His arms.
This man, Jesus, makes her laugh
with His gentlemanly charms.

This man, Jesus, wipes away
all of her tears.
This man, Jesus, puts a stop
to all of her fears.

This man, Jesus, reveals her torment
and causes it to cease.
This man, Jesus, makes her exhale
with His slow, lingering peace.

The Married One looks at her wedding ring
and Jesus looks at His.
The Married One smiles as Jesus whispers
sweet promises in her ears.

*"I'm married unto you,
and I'm preparing you a place."*
He holds her tight,
looks into her eyes,
as He stares into her face.

"I will never leave nor forsake you,"
this man, Jesus, expounds.
The love affair is suddenly interrupted
by a door opening sound.

"What are you smiling about?"
the Creeper asked out loud.
"Just some things my *true* husband said,"
the Married One replied…proud.

An evil man is held captive by his own sins; they are ropes that catch and hold him. He will die for lack of self-control; he will be lost because of his incredible folly. Proverbs 5:15–23, NLT

Therefore take heed to your spirit, and let none deal treacherously against the wife of his youth. Malachi 2:16

"For I hate divorce!" says the Lord…Malachi 2:16, NLT

…In body and spirit you are his (the Lord). Malachi 2:15, NLT

I (Jesus) AM the true vine, and my Father is the husbandman. John 15:5

Turn In Your Captivity!

Obesity Story

I stuffed the last piece of cake in my mouth,
then pondered, "What else can I eat?"
I knew I wasn't hungry,
and shouldn't eat just before I sleep.

But eating had become a habit now,
food was my refuge.
My weight increasing; I hated the scale.
I was becoming morbidly huge.

My clothes no longer fit, so I stayed indoors.
I didn't have anything to wear.
When I would go out,
my feelings would get hurt,
catching the eyes of those who stare.

To work, home, and watch TV
was just about the gist of it.
My self-hatred I refused to address.
My self-pity I laid on thick.

I walked the rooms of my home alone.
Family and friends rarely phoned.
I asked myself, "How did I get like this?"
My part I would eventually have to own.

Why did I choose food to be my savior
rather than Jesus Christ?
Why do I still have desires for toxic
ones to be in my life?

Why do I still mourn for the partner
who left and never returned?
Why do I still try to buy love
when my love others don't try to earn?

"Jesus, help me!" I'm in bondage here!
I desperately need a way out!
Help me to start loving myself
and stop putting all this food to my mouth!

I know this is a sin of the flesh
You can help me to overcome.
But first You've revealed I must deal
with what makes me fear and run."

It's all about not feeling loved,
whether it started as a child or an adult.
This allowed an opening for Satan to enter,
and with his influences run amuck.

Evict Satan from your very being.
Your body is the temple of God.
Satan is a killer, thief and destroyer.
Allowing him to stay is not smart.

Release your pain and fears to Jesus Christ;
He will be your Comforter, you will find.
Reliance upon Jesus, not upon food,
will have a slimming effect in time.

(For many walk...Whose end *is* destruction, whose God *is their* belly, and *whose* glory *is* in their shame, who mind earthly things.) Philippians 3:18–19

And Jesus said unto them, *I am the bread of life: he that cometh to me shall never hunger; and he that believeth on me shall never thrist.* John 6:35

For ye are brought with a price: therefore glorify God in your body, and in your spirit, which are God's. I Corinthians 6:20

…Walk in the Spirit, and ye shall not fulfill the lust of the flesh. Galatians 5:16

I must not become a slave to anything. I Corinthians 6:12, NLT

Will He Marry Me?

"For years I've been in this relationship,
shacking with my man,
yet he repeatedly refuses to marry me.

The damage mental
and emotional abuse is causing,
this too, he repeatedly refuses to see.

Lord, You say the marriage bed is undefiled,
so our *unmarried* bed must be pretty dirty.

No matter how good of a mate I try to be,
I'm made to feel, as a wife, I'm not worthy.

I frequently ask you Lord,
"Why do I live like this?"
The answer You resound within me, "FEAR!"

I thought his love was all I'm worthy of;
no others' love to me would come near.

He said I was ugly, dumb, and crazy;
no others' love I would find.

And he used this type of abuse
to keep me carefully in line.

Lord, You've heard my cries and prayers,
and now convicts me to take a stand.

Even if it means I will lose my warden…
my controller…I mean…my man.

I've been reading the Word,
understanding the liberty
Jesus purchased for me.

I'm now prepared to start the process
of the *turn in my captivity*."

And whosoever will not receive you…shake off the very dust from your feet for a testimony against them. Luke 9:5

(The wicked) Ignore the tunes of the snake charmers no matter how skillfully they play. Psalm 58:5

Except the LORD build the house, they labour in vain that build it…Psalm 127:1

One sinner can destroy much that is good. Ecclesiates 9:18, NLT

…note that man, and have no company with him, that he may be ashamed. II Thessalonians 3:14

Domestic Violence Story

"Are you ok?" my Girlfriend asked,
as I quickly turned to hide my face.
"Yeah, I was cleaning the bathroom and fell,
that's why I'm in a daze."

"What's wrong with your eye?" my Girlfriend asked,
as she moved in for a closer inspection.
"Girl, what are you talking about, I'm fine!"
I said with an irritated interjection.

"Ooh! You have a black eye!" my Girlfriend exclaimed
in my house quiet and still.
I pleaded within myself, 'Don't let her figure it out,
that this came from my husband, Phil.'

"I know you're not letting that man
hit and beat up on you," was her next reply.
"No, I told you what happened.
Don't come over here causing trouble,"
I added to the lie.

"Now I know why you didn't answer the door
when I came over twice.
I told you not to marry that man.
You're too good to be his wife.

He wants to keep you under lock and key,
while he roams fancy free.
He doesn't show you any respect."
"Now stop right there!" I tried to interject.

"He wants his food on the table by five,
still hot and steaming,
when through the door he arrives.

This man, he can't keep a job,
and leaves you to pay all the bills.
Don't act all surprised,
you know I'm telling the truth
about your husband, Phil.

He doesn't want you to get ahead in life,
and keeps you under his thumb.
You remember how he acted
when you wanted to go back to school.
I would've left the dirty bum!

And had the nerve to say
you couldn't visit your family.
Nope, I wouldn't have any man like that around me.

And does he still want sex two
and three times a day?
I wouldn't give him nothing after hitting me,
no way!"

"I hear what you're saying Girlfriend,
the things you said are right.
But I'm in a spiritual warfare for my marriage;
I'm not ready to give up the fight.

I'm praying for Phil's deliverance night and day.
Believe it or not, that is why I stay.

If Phil continues in his violent way
and is not swayed to my side,
from him I will have to separate;
we will no longer together abide.

I know Jesus does not want me in bondage.
He died that I may be free.
For where the Spirit of the Lord resides,
there is Liberty.

If I depart, I will await from God
the answer to my future.
Do I remain departed,
or later be reconciled to Phil?
But only if Phil has learned to let peace be still.

Only if he can prove to me
his violent ways have ceased.
Only if Phil is following
after the love of God and peace.

The bible says the husband
can be won by the wife's conversation.
If I let my light shine,
a holy marriage could be my consolation.

For who knows the part I may play
in helping Phil to be saved?
He may give his life to Jesus,
as life for him, Jesus gave."

This is true, and everyone should accept it. We work hard and suffer much in order that people will believe the truth, for our hope is in the living God, who is the Savior of all people, and particularly of those who believe. I Timothy 4:9–10, NLT

Because sentencing against an evil work is not executed speedily…Ecclesiates 8:11

Not because we have not power, but to make ourselves an ensample...II Thessalonians 3:9

Be not over much wicked, neither be thou foolish: why shouldest thou die before thy time? Ecclesiates 7:17

Because they have no changes, therefore they fear not God. Psalm 55:19

...I withdrew myself from them, but they went right on sinning. Isaiah 57:17, NLT

Wicked People

There are sinful,
wicked people in this world,
who just push God's truth away.

This truth is instinctively
written in their hearts
is what the bible has to say.

All God made
have clearly been seen
from the time the world was created.

The wicked have no excuse
for not knowing God,
but yet they're glad to debate it.

They know God,
but won't worship Him as God,
or even give Him thanks.

Their minds are dark
and their wicked acts
in the nostrils of God stank.

Instead of believing
what they know is the truth,
they deliberately chose to believe lies.

They worship things God made,
but not the Creator,
causing Him to be dissatisfied.

God does not force us.
He allows us to choose our will.

He is not a God of oppression.
Our freedom He will not try to steal.

That's why God releases the wicked
to the evilness of their minds.

Their lives are full of wickedness,
of every kind:

sin, greed, hate, envy, murder,
fighting, deception, intent to harm,
gossip, backstabbers,
haters of God, boldly disrespectful,
proud, boastful, disobedient
to parents, refuse to understand,
break their promises, are heartless
and unforgiving.

They are fully aware of God's death penalty,
yet on wickedness continue to feast.

And just as God,
there are some
you may have to release.

But release them with love,
never avenge yourself.
Justice is left to God.

This is the way you guard
against wickedness
infiltrating your heart.

For their being released

may cause them shame,
for their mistreatment of you.

Resulting in them opening their minds,
and cease pushing away God's truth.

All the ways of a man are clean in his own eyes; but the LORD weigheth the spirits. Proverbs 16:2

For men shall be lovers of their own selves, covetous, boasters, proud, blasphemers, disobedient to parents, unthankful, unholy, Without natural affection, trucebreakers, false accusers, incontinent, fierce, despisers of those that are good, Traitors, heady, highminded, lovers of pleasures more than lovers of God; Having a form of godliness, but denying the power thereof: from such turn away…Ever learning, and never able to come to the knowledge of the truth…these also resist the truth: men of corrupt minds, reprobates concerning the faith…II Timothy 3:2–8

Worship The Lord God Only

We shall walk after the Lord our God,
fear Him, keep His commandments,
serve Him, and cleave unto Him.

Take heed to yourself,
that your heart be not deceived,
and you turn aside, serve other gods,
and worship them.

We shall not do those things;
for every abomination God hates,
to other gods they have been done.

Some affect their families by their ungodly worship,
offering their daughters as sacrifice,
even their own sons.

Therefore shall you abide in God's Word.
Bind it upon your hand for a sign.

Say, "Lord, write them upon
the door posts of my house,
and on everything that's of mine."

If a brother, son, daughter,
friend, or even spouse,
say, "Let us go and other gods do serve."

We shall not hearken,
or pity them;
instead rebuke,
using the power of God's Word.

Take heed to yourself
that you be not snared,
for their gods will be destroyed before you.

Do not inquire after their idols,
wondering how they serve,
but to the Trinity remain true.

God said,
"I set before you this day a blessing and a curse.
A blessing, if you obey my commandments,
and a curse if you turn aside."

But many still follow and bow to other gods,
provoking the Lord's anger to arise.

They practice cutting themselves,
witchcraft, sorcery,
and making baldness
between their eyes for the dead.

The heavens would celebrate,
with God as the strongest voice,
if they made the *turn in their captivity*
as Jesus led.

Some turn their worship to angels
and the Virgin Mary,
whose holiness and image please us.

But like the angel said,
"Don't worship me,
I'm a servant of God…
who testifies faith in Jesus."

These beings are helpers of God,
just as you have been assigned to be.

Their assignment may be of a greater work,
but unto you, an assignment, God also decree.

We are not to rob from Jesus the honor
and credit He is due.

For He is the Way, the Truth, and the Life,
the *only* One you should work through.

There are hypocrites,
whose worship of God is a farce,
replacing God's commands
with their own man-made teachings.

These people honor God with their words,
but not their hearts.
It's their own man-made rules
they're preaching.

It may seem that strong devotion to people
would cause them to show
love, justice and respect.

But the bible says this passivity
do not conquer evil thoughts…
against wickedness it has no effect.

We're not to be *will worshippers*…
worshipping the wills of humans
and sacrificing to them our life.

Beware lest you're spoiled
through philosophy,
and traditions of men,
   …and not after Christ.

But when individuals corrupt themselves;
and cease not from their own doings,
nor from their stubborn ways.

God said, *"I will not
drive evil out from before you,
they shall be as thorns and snare...
these gods whom you obeyed.*

*You have forsaken me,
wherefore I will deliver you no more
from your degradation.*

*Go and cry unto the gods
whom you have chosen;
let them deliver you
in the time of your tribulation."*

Through their captivity,
God may prove
whether they will keep the way of the Lord
to walk therein.

God will observe
whom they worship and love the best,
if the Father, Son, and Holy Ghost
are who they defend.

If they make the *turn in their captivity*,
and stop worshipping other gods...
there shall cleave nothing of the curse.

The Lord shall have compassion
and multiply them,
as He wanted to do at first.

Turn In Your Captivity!

They must overthrow their idol altars,
break their pillars,
and burn their groves with fire.

They must hew down their graven images,
destroy idol names,
display the Trinity for all to admire.

…For they have forgotten the Lord their God and wandered far from his ways. "My wayward children," says the Lord, "come back to me, and I will heal your wayward hearts." Jeremiah 3:21–22, NLT

Whosoever denieth the Son, the same hath not the Father: (but) he that acknowledgeth the Son hath the Father also. 1 John 2:23

…And it is the Spirit that beareth witness, because the Spirit is truth. For there are three that bear record in heaven, the Father, the Word (Jesus Christ), and the Holy Ghost: and these three agree in one. I John 5:6–7

Witchcraft, Sorcery In Our Society

Many are in oppressive circumstances
due to manipulators in society
who have the upper hand,
because they're not fighting fair.

They elicit power from
outside the power of God,
which many know not of,
nor even think to care.

But it's this lack of knowledge
that's causing their captive demise,
and the failing of their tests.

We must learn the wiles of the devil,
how Satan and his team work,
so we can spiritually fight our best.

The reality of witchcraft
and sorcery in our society is real.

The destruction of our godly destiny,
and God's glory are what they're trying to kill.

They can be your daily trouble,
but many of you do not know,
because you're not taught these things.

Many of you are in severe grief
from being oppressed by others,
who are simply not just being mean.

If you sense a monitoring spirit…
a spectator's eye,
a spell affecting matters in your life.

Learn The Jesus Way skills and techniques.
Don't allow your life to be the ultimate sacrifice.

Some particular birds like coming to your home,
and you wonder why.

You sleep and find animals pursue you in the night,
causing you to awake with a cry.

Those birds…those snakes…those scorpions…
those headaches that come to torment in the night.

Those witches…those veils…those sorcerers…
those spells that come to challenge and subdue your fight.

But there is never any witch
or sorcerer to fear.

Through Jesus,
we tread over all their powers;
none of their hurts can come near.

Witchcraft is exercising control
over an individual.
This is not the kind of authority given from God.

God does not force control,
He allows free will;
so knowing the difference between the two
is not hard.

There is black witchcraft, white witchcraft,
and witchcraft that is blind.

Discern your life for any signs,
for witchcraft manipulation
you may find.

Black witchcraft aggressively afflicts,
to take your portion,
and stop you from progressing.

Their goal is to move your landmarks,
kill your destiny,
and destroy your godly confessing.

White witches are self-righteous,
covering their evil in nice packages
is how they play.

They won't kill you like a rat,
but in a slow, merciful way.

Blind witches make the person
carry out witchcraft acts,
using remote control from afar.

They play with people like toys,
making them do things
both evil and bizarre.

Sorcery is the use of a symbol
from something that belongs to you,
in order to afflict.

What carries your name,
what bears your life,
a pin, they will use to stick.

Receive power against every evil principality
in the heavenly places,
and in the earth.

This power is received
through the blood of Jesus Christ,
for without Him, we're only dirt.

Release the power in His blood
to pull you out of the circles of Satan's snares.

Release His blood to
put out the eye
that dares to follow your everywhere.

Invite God to make a protection covenant for you
with the things He created.
You, they will recognize and obey.

If anyone attempts to place a curse on you,
God's creation will rebuke, reverse,
and scatter it away.

You will lie down safely,
and be free of evil dreams.

Because you and your territory
are witchcraft and sorcery clean.

Jesus answered, *I have not a devil;* John 8:49

…who hath bewitched you, that ye should not obey the truth…?
Galatians 3:1

For rebellion *is as* the sin of witchcraft…I Samuel 15:23

Eat not the bread of *him that hath* an evil eye, neither desire thou his dainty meats: For as he thinketh in his heart, so is he: Eat and drink, saith he to thee; but his heart *is* not with thee. Proverbs 23:6

…I would have you wise unto that which is good, and simple concerning evil. And the God of peace shall bruise Satan under your feet shortly. Romans 16:19–20

There shall not be found among you any one that maketh his son or his daughter to pass through the fire, or that useth divination, or an observer of times, or an enchanter, or a witch. Or a charmer, or a consulter with familiar spirits, or a wizard, or a necromancer. For all that do these things are an abomination unto the Lord: and because of these abominations the Lord thy God doth drive them out from before thee. Deuteronomy 18:10–12

Stand In The Gap

In the context of a dream:
in a corner at the side of my house,
a gruesome scene was seen.
It appeared a helpless mutt
was being ferociously devoured
by three other dogs that were mean.

The foolish dog willingly lay on the ground,
allowing himself to be lunch.
I tried to shoo them away from him,
but they continued to crunch and munch.

Even though they were killing him,
he took pleasure in the three.
He willingly chose not to say,
"Get away from me!"

I picked up rocks to throw at them,
but the deceived mutt invited them in deeper.
They totally disregarded my threats,
for this feast was definitely a keeper.

He didn't try to fight them off,
but surrendered to *their* will.
He himself was a punisher…a predator,
and enjoyed the taste of kill.

He himself was a willing participant
in gangster and mafia techniques.
Proud to learn evil skills,

Sandra Wilson

in exchange of his body
and soul for their meat.

The biggest of the eating dogs,
slowly turned and looked at me.
"You have no power here.
You can't make us stop,
for he is willingly."

"I'm not deceived by you,
as that mutt over there.
I have the power of Jesus Christ,
so rebuking me, don't you dare!

For others I stand in the gap
and make up a hedge,
just as Jesus did for me.
I will pray for the willing mutt's
deliverance from evil,
and for the *turn in his captivity!*

For whether he will hear or not,
as God's Gatekeeper,
I will warn him of his ways.
For you do not have the last word.
The last word is that…
"Jesus Saves!"

And I will appoint over them (the wicked) four kinds, saith the LORD: the sword to slay, and the dogs to tear, and the fowls of the heaven, and the beasts of the earth, to devour and destroy. Jeremiah 15:3

...and he (Jesus Christ) bare the sin of many, and made intercession for the transgressors. Isaiah 53:12

And *that* they may recover themselves out of the snare of the devil, who are taken captive by him at his will. II Timothy 2:26

The effectual fervent prayer of a righteous man (woman) availeth much. James 5:16

...and thou shalt be called, The repairer of the breach, The restorer of paths to dwell in. Isaiah 58:12

Mental and Emotional Oppression Story

She timidly asked,
"Honey, is it okay if I go to the movies
with my girlfriend?"

"No," was the blunt reply.
"Why not honey?
I won't be gone long."

"When I say no,
don't be questioning me
and asking me why!"

Anger and desperation rises inside,
but she dare not let him see.

She goes to her secret place of prayer,
and falls down on her knees.

"Lord, this is the man
who promised to always love and cherish me.

My spirit is grieving;
my mind in torment,
yet he refuses to see.

He acts more like a warden,
and insists on doing me wrong.

He treats me like I'm a child,
as if I'm not even grown.

He defines his manhood by being
controlling and domineering.

His motto,
"You're not being submissive enough,"
and wants me always fearing.

He lays down rules
that seem just for me.
I'm not allowed to make a mistake.

Being with him, I'm losing my identity
and starting to feel like a fake.

He demands a wife who's obedient and submissive.
Jesus, You know I've tried to be just that.

But where's the respect and submissiveness
I'm to receive?
I'm being given low self-esteem,
which is making me fat!

If I'm allowed to go out,
when I return,
I must be prepared for the interrogation.

"Who was there?"
"Who did you talk to?"
have to be answered
without showing irritation.

The Word says,
A husband and wife are to submit one to another,
not the one-sidedness I face.

Sandra Wilson

Husbands are to love their wives
as they love themselves
is the honor, to me, the Word place.

For God has not given me the spirit of fear.
I shall know the truth,
and the truth shall make me free.

Mutual love and respect in my marriage
is what will bring peace to my husband and me.

Extra problems come with marriage.
I have to dig deeper in You, Jesus,
to make it work.

For the Christian wife
brings holiness to her marriage.
Because of The Jesus Way,
my husband might convert.

I will declare the Word,
taking my stand,
while showering him
with patience, love and respect.

I will pray for him…
his deliverance,
while allowing time
from his oppressive ways to defect.

There is the chance
he could detest my stance
from captivity to be free.

There is the chance
he could leave the marriage,
choosing to abandon me.

But it's written,
if the husband or wife who's an unbeliever
insists on leaving…let them walk away.

In such cases,
the Christian husband or wife
is not required with them to stay.

But if my husband is willing to continue with me,
a holy marriage could be my reward.

I'm no longer fearful of my future,
but in The Jesus Way heading forward.

I've learned from my oppressive state,
God is the only One who can truly affirm us.

And You, Jesus Christ, is the only One
whom I should truly place all my trust."

They that forsake the law (of God) praise the wicked: but such as keep the law contend with them. Proverbs 28:4

Not giving heed to…fables, and commandments of men, that turn from the truth. Titus 1:14

Take no part in the worthless deeds of evil and darkness; instead, rebuke and expose them...But when the light shines on them, it becomes clear how evil these things are. And where your light shines, it will expose their evil deeds. Ephesians 5:11, 13–14, NLT

Yet count *him* not as an enemy, but admonish *him* as a brother. II Thessalonians 3:15

All Have Sinned Versus Wickedness

The bible says only God is good,
and there is not a single person
in all the earth,
who is always good and never sin.

But our sins can be covered daily
by the blood of Jesus,
and the mercy of God,
a truth on which we depend!

We all make many mistakes,
and it's impossible
for offenses not to come.

Whatever is done without faith,
and even foolish thoughts
are sins we all commit…
not some.

So what is the difference
between sinning and wickedness?
When Christians sin are they evil and wicked?
What makes someone evil when they sin,
and another not?

The difference between the two
is discussed in some detail,
so if you're committing evil and wickedness,
by the delivering power of Jesus, you can stop.

Sandra Wilson

The bible does make a differentiation
in the various forms of sin.

But it's Jesus Christ's cleansing
which enables us over sin to win.

The wicked perform deliberate sins,
but the Christian's sin is by ignorant error.

We should speak truth
about the types of sin we commit,
as we look at ourselves in the mirror.

Those with deliberate sins
have hatred in their hearts.
They knew what they were doing.
They set it up!

With sinning by ignorant error,
their actions caused an offense;
but they were unaware,
and their hearts were still with love.

A biblical example
is of a man chopping wood;
the axe head flew off
and killed his neighbor.

He should have inspected
before he chopped,
but because of innocence in his heart,
he still received God's favor.

Then there are persistent sinners
versus those who sin
as a result of being provoked.

They pick with you,
and when you react out of character,
they say, "It's just a joke."

Persistent sinning is a result of
persistent character.
In these individuals, no integrity lies.

They repeat the same sins,
even after God and others
have given them numerous tries.

Persistent sinners are the same ones
who the Righteous have to
persistently confront and rebuke.

*"How terrible it will be for those
who cause others to sin,"*
is the favor Jesus gives;
because of temptation challenges
He went through.

The wicked
will attempt to hide their sins;
whereas there are those sinners
who readily confess.

The wicked
will accuse, condemn,
and torment others about their faults,
but their own shortcomings not address.

Those who confess receive cleansing,
due to the blood of Jesus;
their spiritual garments remain white.

But those who do not confess,
their sins are not forgiven;
so their garments become black as the night.

There are some sinners,
who are controlled by their sins,
yet others who refuse it dominion.

The wicked are ones
who allow sin's control,
and when warned,
refuse to hear the opinion.

The Christian prays,
"Order my steps in thy word, O Lord.
Let not any iniquity rule over me."

They want to live with godly integrity,
whereas, the wicked says,
"As a rebel against God, let me be!"

What sums it up for God is the heart.
Is it hard and dark,
or does it remain soft and sincere?

The wicked,
walking in their own imaginations,
cause the guilt curse on their hands
to be severe.

The curse causeless shall not come!
The Righteous knows this,
and protects his heart
by doing what's right.

The curse will not cleave to him…
the curse meant for those evil;
because of the innocence of his hands
in the Lord's sight.

Again and again,
the guilt of the wicked cries out,
but of their sins they're not ashamed.

They refuse to set their house in God's order,
and give to Jesus their captivity pain.

The wicked should follow
the Christian's example:
daily ask for forgiveness,
and allow Jesus to tear
the guilt layers of their sins away.

From guilt captivity they will be freed,
their ears will be open to heed;
and The Jesus Way
they will learn to gladly obey.

The wicked are sinners
who have grievous sins,
causing severe torment
and sufferings for others.

Then there are those
who caused someone an offense,
but it doesn't create a feel of smother.

The Word explains:
if his ways are always grievous,
he shall be beaten with many strikes.

But if he's innocent of grievous sins,
he shall be chastised,
but with fewer swipes.

Son of man, when the land sinneth against me by trespassing grievously, then will I (the Lord) stretch out mine hand upon it…Ezekiel 14:13

But the destruction will come if you will not hear…and if this refusal of God is your manner consistently…And you refuse to obey God's voice. Jeremiah 22:21, NLT

Dear friends, if we deliberately continue sinning after we have received a full knowledge of the truth (Jesus Christ), there is no other sacrifice that will cover these sins. Hebrews 10:26, NLT

Then said the Lord unto me, Pray not for this people for *their* good. Jeremiah 14:11

All unrighteousness is sin: and there is a sin not unto death. I John 5:17

I (Jesus) pray for them: I pray not for the world, but for them which thou (Father God) hast given me; for they are thine. John 17:9

Yield Not To Temptation

I sometimes resist surrendering
to my husband, as unto God.
It's not that I'm frequently like this,
because I do try mightily hard.

It's just on occasion times,
I yield to my irritation spirit,
and the fight would come on.
Then all the order times
are in threat of being destroyed,
I had victoriously sown.

Why can't I keep it straight?
Why can't I do it right?
My husband says I love to not submit.
He says I love to fight.

I admit I try to fight against injustices,
I feel he does to me.
My irritation arises,
and I demand at himself,
he looks and sees.

But this way never works.
In my face it violently explodes.
I'm left to try and regain the peace,
my irritation tried to erode.

I must remember the fight
is not against flesh and blood,

Sandra Wilson

aligning myself to The Jesus Way.
Taking my fleshly emotion
out of the reaction equation,
is the only way peace will stay.

I know I can conquer this irritation
and force it to flee from me.
I know I can do it,
because through the Word,
I have the victory.

"Yield not to temptation,
for yielding is sin."
God would not have commanded
what I could not possibly win.

"Do not speak evil of anyone who heads over you,"
in the bible is what I read.
The prophet, Paul, made this statement,
as he apologized for what he said.

I can not submit to my husband,
until I've learned to fully submit to God.
Developing the skill of submission,
will make my marital life blessed,
and less hard.

So to God's Word,
I transform my yielding focus,
as I kill my flesh day by day.
Stable unity with my husband is achieved,
through living The Jesus Way.

My husband is godly placed over me.
I'm not permitted to teach and instruct my head.
My husband is taught through his answering to God,
and from the Christian light I shed.

I pray God will teach my husband
to be supportive of my quest to grow.
For the order God demands of my husband
is that he nourish and cherish me, you know?

I'm glad I serve a God that's just,
and not one-sided in the matter.
For it's The Jesus Way, Truth and Life
that put an end to my irritation's chatter.

Submit yourselves therefore to God. Resist the devil, and he will flee from you. James 4:7

…you wives must accept the authority of your husbands, even those who refuse to accept the Good News. Your godly lives will speak to them better than any words. I Peter 3:1, NLT

But I do not discard the law of God; I obey the law of Christ. I Corinthians 9:21, NLT

That thou mayest walk in the way of good men, and keep the path of the righteous. Proverbs 2:20

Responsible Forgiveness

I won't forgive him, I vowed to myself.
I will always hold a grudge.
"Will you forgive me?" he asked.
As I stared straight ahead, I shrugged.

Shrugging to say,
I don't know if I will.
Shrugging to say,
peace is not going to be still.

I'm going to allow
much frustration to vent.
I'm going to cause
much hell to be bent.

All because I chose not to forgive,
I'm going to make your life
difficult to live.

I'm going to make
you wish you were never born.
I'm going to get joy
out of seeing your face forlorn.

Jesus Christ forgave us;
therefore, we all have that responsibility too.
Responsible forgiveness
is what we're supposed to do.

The responsibility to say,
"I love you regardless of."
The responsibility is there because of
God's command for us to love.

To love our neighbor
as we love ourselves.
To not take our forgiveness
and place it upon shelves.

But to practice it daily
and have it available in our life.
To put into action,
so forgiveness won't have to be asked twice.

If we confess our sins, he (Jesus Christ) is faithful and just to forgive us *our* sins, and to cleanse us from all unrighteousness. I John 1:9

Cast away from you all your transgressions, whereby you have transgressed: and make you a new heart and a new spirit. Ezekiel 18:31

...ye *ought* rather to forgive *him*, and comfort *him*, lest perhaps such a one should be swallowed up with overmuch sorrow. Wherefore I beseech you that ye would confirm *your* love toward him...Lest Satan should get an advantage of us: for we are not ignorant of his devices. II Corinthians 2:7–11

*(Although we must forgive a persistent sinner, our forgiveness of him or her does not mean that we are now

forced to remain a partner and a part of his or her sins. It does not mean that we allow ourselves to be open to persistent insults and injuries. We have a God-given right to self-protect and self-respect. We have a God-given command to develop the skill of release (forgiving, separating, and continuing to walk in love).

*(If an abuser repents, does that mean God's vengeance for all the victim's endured afflictions is cancelled?)…thou wast a God that forgavest them, though thou tookest vengeance of their inventions. Psalm 99:8

If any man's work shall be burned, he shall suffer loss: but he himself shall be saved…I Corinthians 3:15

Why Do You Watch Over Me Lord?

Why do you watch over me Lord?
To teach you the skills of life

Why do you watch over me Lord?
To guide you in being a godly wife

Why do you watch over me Lord?
To keep Satan beneath
and you above

Why do you watch over me Lord?
To teach you how to walk
in peace and in love

Why do you watch over me Lord?
Because I care for you

Why do you watch over me Lord?
To give you victory
over the sins that you do

Why do you watch over me Lord?
Because it's about obedience to Me,
not ungodly sacrifice

Why do you watch over me Lord?
To show you how to be a godly wife

Why do you watch over me Lord?
Because to your husband,
you break rank,
and make his marital life hard

Why do you watch over me Lord?
To instill peace,
to show you where you fit,
and what is your part

Why do you watch over me Lord?
Again, you're slow to understand

Why do you watch over me Lord?
You need skills to be with a husband-man

Why do you watch over me Lord?
Again, I will tell you thrice

Why do you watch over me Lord?
To give you skills in life,
on being a godly wife

"Look, God is all powerful. Who is a teacher like him?
Job 36:22, NLT

If trouble come upon them and they are enslaved and afflicted, he takes the trouble to show them the reason. He shows them their sins, for they have behaved proudly. He gets their attention and says they must turn away from evil.
Job 36:8–10, NLT

Turn In Your Captivity!

Why are you so angry with the one you chose as king?
1. You have renounced your covenant with him,
   for you have thrown his crown in the dust.
2. You have broken down the walls protecting him
   and laid in ruins every fort defending him.
3. Everyone who comes along has robbed him
   while his neighbors mock.
4. You have strengthened his enemies against him
   and made them all rejoice.
5. You have made his sword useless
   and have refused to help him in battle.
6. You have ended his splendor
   and overturned his throne.
7. You have made him old before his time
   and publicly disgraced him.
   Psalm 89:38–45

...And now look, your house is left to you, empty and desolate.
Matthew 23:37–38

And I find more bitter than death the woman; whose heart *is* snares and nets, *and* her hands *as* bands: Ecclesiastes 7:26

But I suffer not a woman to teach, nor to usurp authority over the man (her own husband)...I Timothy 2:12

I Hit Him!

I hit him in the face,
then returned to inflict repeated blows.
He did nothing in his defense,
as I aimed precariously for his nose.

My licks were meant to be
the teacher to get him to admit his lie.
My licks were meant to be
the rod to whip for his ridiculous alibi.

But violence just doesn't stop at physical,
it leads to other things.
Violence came also out of my mouth,
causing words hurtful and mean.

He protected his head as best he could,
as my arms flailed away.
It was intended as a message,
'I will not tolerate lies,'
but I was going about it the wrong way.

My breath were words of bluff,
I knew I couldn't control his will.
But the fear inside,
driving the anger,
refused to let peace be still.

Through all my ranting and raving,
he never said a word.
After all my fleshly
emotions were spent,
my spirit was left disturbed.

Disturbed I had allowed
the devil to enter my home.
Disturbed I let my godly shield down
and Satan permitted to roam.

I knew the devil only comes
to kill, steal, and destroy;
I had to be wise to his ways.
But I let my guard down
and was carrying on,
as if I wasn't even saved.

Once the violent acts and words are out there,
there's no way to take them back.
For seed, time, and harvest;
for reaper of what you sow,
is taking names and keeping track.

His not returning violence for violence,
is what convicted me to the core.
His not returning violence for violence,
made me see I needed The Jesus Way more.

I plead temporary insanity.
I forgot not to fight against
flesh and blood.
If we aren't careful,
Satan will have us killing, stealing from,
and destroying the ones we love.

Violent force should be reserved to fight
powers of darkness,
and wicked spirits in the heavenly realm.
Guarding and taking back
what belongs to us, through Jesus,
is the fight to be used against them.

We should not try to control
and manipulate someone to be,
do, and act as we see fit.
But be The Jesus Way example,
and allow God to handle it.

Then Simon Peter having a sword drew it, and smote the high priest's servant, and cut off his right ear...Then said Jesus unto Peter, *Put up thy sword into the sheath*...John 18:11

Wisdom *is* better than weapons of war: Ecclesiastes 9:18

...so fight I, not as one that beateth the air: But I keep under my body, and bring *it* into subjection: lest that by any means, when I have preached to others, I myself should be a castaway. I Corinthians 9:26–27

Abandonment Story

Upon entering the house I sensed a strange silence,
the rooms were utterly still.
As I glanced around I noticed vacant areas,
as more information the rooms revealed.

What happened to the TV?
Why is that closet bare?
What happened to the throw on the couch?
I stood numb and could do nothing but stare.

The shoes always aligned next to the bed
are no longer seen.
What has happened to my partner in life?
Are we no longer a team?

Did the moving van come and fill its chamber
with my life I thought sweet and true?
Why did the van come when I was safely tucked away?
A plan secretly thought through.

The full impact of what I'm privy to,
is hitting me like a ton of bricks.
I cannot believe my partner would do this to me!
I cannot believe I've been tricked!

The serpent-like word, *"Abandonment,"*
slivered from my head
and slowly down my inner being.
I could not measure the pain of reality…
the reality of what my eyes were now seeing.

Sandra Wilson

"Jesus!" echoed through the vacant spaces
as I yelled to the top of my lungs.
"Help me," is all my wounded spirit could muster.
Thank God I knew where my strength comes from.

As soon as the breath of the spoken words
started to migrate through the room.
The love of Jesus filled the vacated spaces
and not a moment too soon.

"I am with you always,
even unto the ends of the earth.
I will never leave nor forsake you."
I'm glad Jesus could see my love worth!

They went out from us, but they were not of us; for if they had been of us, they would *no doubt* have continued with us: but *they went out*, that they might be made manifest that they were not all of us. I John 2:19

…and yet I am not alone, because the Father is with me.
John 16:32

Take heed that ye be not deceived…go ye not therefore after them.
Luke 21:8

Can someone break their sworn treaties like that and get away with it? No! For whoever despised and broke the treaty, there will be no escape…I (God) will punish him for breaking my covenant and despising the solemn oath he made in my name. Ezekiel 17:15-19, NLT

Turn In Your Captivity!

(unless her husband has been unfaithful)...let her remain single...I Corinthians 7:10–16, NLT

(unless her husband has been unfaithful) A wife is married to her husband as long as he lives. I Corinthians 7:39, NLT

(unless her husband has been unfaithful)...*whoso marrieth her which is put away doth commit adultery.* Matthew 19:9

...a man who divorces his wife and marries another commits adultery—-unless his wife has been unfaithful. Matthew 19:9, NLT

Could It Be?

I let him come back into my life,
although he had abandoned me
so many times before.

I let him come back into my life,
but after today…no more.

Why is today different
from all the other days?

Why is today's difference
forcing me to change my ways?

Could it be
he took me to the shopping mall,
and deceitfully left me there?

Could it be
he forced me to recognize his deep hate,
and his lack, to me, of care?

Could it be
I listened to his pleased phone call
of "Goodbye, I'm gone?"

Could it be
I listened to him joyfully say,
"Find another means
of transport home?"

Could it be
I saw him in the distance…
watching…as he spoke
…enjoying my pain?

Could it be
I finally faced the truth,
'This man is trying to drive me insane?'

Could it be
he abandoned me at my weakest
…unable to work
and in a neck brace?

Could it be
I finally accepted,
with him I will never
be at peace or feel safe?

Could it be
the fullness of the shame
hit me like a ton of bricks?

Could it be
I finally said from my gut,
"Enough is enough,"
as I waited for my sister…
in my neck brace…feeling sick?

There is an evil *which* I have seen under the sun, as an error *which* proceedeth from the ruler: Ecclesiastes 10:5

The beginning of the words of his mouth *is* foolishness: and the end of his talk *is* mischievous madness. Ecclesiastes 10:13

It is as sport to a fool to do mischief: Proverbs 10:23

It does no good to charm a snake after it has bitten you. Ecclesiastes 10:11, NLT

Ever learning, and never able to come to the knowledge of the truth. II Timothy 3:7

Confidence in an unfaithful man in time of trouble *is like* a broken tooth, and a foot out of joint. Proverbs 25:19

A Sister's Love

I was numb, bewildered, and in pain…
then a sister's love stepped in.

I felt all the troubles of this world,
on me, it rained…
then a sister's love stepped in.

She soothed my anxiety with her loving words,
speaking, "I'm going to take care of you."

This sister's love was a gift from God,
and I give it all the honor
and respect it's due.

She transported me to her safe haven,
and watched movies with me
till I smiled.

She prepared sustenance for my body,
and sat and had sister-talk with me
for awhile.

The sweet smell of my sister's home
rose to greet me
as I snuggled under the covers deep.

"Thank you God for my sister's love and care,"
I whispered,
as I turned to slumber and sleep.

They attacked me at a moment when I was weakest, but the LORD upheld me. He led me to a place of safety; he rescued me because he delights in me. Psalm 18:18–19, NLT

I Commend unto you…our sister, which is a servant of the church…That ye receive her in the Lord, as becometh saints, and that ye assist her in whatsoever business she hath need of you: for she has been a succourer of many, and of myself also. Romans 16:1–2

The Avenging Angel

For every slap you're slapped,
God appoints the evil angel
to avenge for you.
When others say,
"You're a fool for forgiving,"
God will avenge their words too.

There are angels God has created
to do evil on your behalf.
So release the offense to God;
don't allow your hurt
to last and last.

God's commandments
do not make you a fool.
To you it will bring no shame.
For everything God tells you to do,
He's made provisions
heaven and earth will proclaim.

When God tells you to forgive,
He's already made provisions
for the evil angel to avenge.
What triggers that angel for you
is your not seeking your own revenge.

It's turning the world's so called,
'foolishness,' into your own strength.
For your enemies will find instead
it's their strength that went.

Sandra Wilson

Because they have been forgiven,
they think they have the upper hand.
No, you've just set them up
for the heavens to take your stand!

The Lord has made everything for his own purposes, even the wicked for punishment. Proverbs 16:4, NLT

Evil pursueth sinners: but to the righteous good shall be repaid. Proverbs 13:21

Evil shall slay the wicked: Psalm 34:21

The Van Back!

I wanted to get my new van back!
My husband had taken it
and left me to pay the note!
My name alone on the finance,
I was oppressed
by possibly going financially broke!

I wanted to hunt him down
and force him to his knees!
Things I wanted to do to him…
I couldn't because to God it wouldn't please.

I had vowed total surrender,
and I knew this was my test.
It took constant prayer and submission,
but I was determined by God to be blessed.

When I would think thoughts of revenge!
Jesus would say, *"When you surrender
there are no acts of defend."*

When I would think, 'I'm going,
and him I will find!'
Jesus would say,
"Put those thoughts of revenge out your mind.

Surrendering means standing still
and watching the awesomeness of God.
Doing nothing and accepting the pain,
at first, was awfully hard.

Sandra Wilson

Then as the days went by
and I constrained the will of my flesh to obey.
I gained such a joy and peace,
it became easier in The Jesus Way.

Now when I think about my situation,
I pray, "Lord, let Your will be done."
I'm stronger for going through
and having the faith,
all my battles will be won.

Why do ye not rather take wrong? why do ye not rather *suffer yourselves* to be defrauded? I Corinthians 6:7

...when things are taken away from you, don't try to get them back. Luke 6:30, NLT

...*Suffer it to be so now: for thus it becometh us to fulfil all righteousness.* Matthew 3:15

God has led you away from danger, giving you freedom. You have prospered in a wide and pleasant valley. But you are too obsessed with judgment on the godless. Don't worry, justice will be upheld. But watch out, or you may be seduced with wealth. Don't let yourself be bribed into sin. Could all your wealth and mighty efforts keep you from distress? Do not long for the cover of night, for that is when people will be destroyed. Be on guard! Turn back from evil, for it was to prevent you from getting into a life of evil that God sent this suffering. Job 36:16–21, NLT

Ye shall not *need* to fight in this *battle*: set yourselves, stand ye *still*, and see the salvation of the Lord with you…
II Chronicles 20:17

…the word of God is not bound. II Timothy 2:9

Look-Out For Love

She rose up early before the crack of dawn
to assist me in some detective work.
My husband, her brother-in-law,
had run off with the new van,
and we were trying to find that jerk.

Her eyes scanned the streets
with a determination
to help me out of this captive bind.
I looked at her profile, smiled and thought,
'She's so great, this sister of mine.'

This one time of searching,
trying myself to fight,
convicted me to the core.
I told my sister, "I'm going home now.
I'm not going to try
and do this on my own anymore."

I had vowed to surrender to God,
and let peace be still.
God had vowed victory
in my struggle,
so I re-constrained my flesh to his will.

And I was with you in weakness, and in fear, and in much trembling. I Corinthians 2:3

For the love of Christ constraineth us; because we thus judge…II Corinthians 5:14

…Abide not in the hold; depart, and get thee into the land…I Samuel 22:5

At First

At first,
he said he wanted us to be so close;
he wanted me always physically there.

At first,
we would go to dinner,
then to the movies;
our togetherness was everywhere.

At first,
I thought he was so loving
and for me he truly cared.

At first,
he would laugh at my jokes,
tell me I was beautiful,
and lovingly played with my hair.

At first,
he was such a gentleman,
always opening my doors
and pulling out my chair.

But the second season time approached,
and much too rapidly it came.

I'm perplexed and in a daze,
my man no longer
treats me as his dame.

I thought
he was the sunshine of my life,
but too quickly came the storms and rain.

I was left soaked
without an umbrella,
as he said in disgust,
I no longer looked the same.

When I knocked on the door
to come out of the weather,
he just continued
to snack and watch the game.

Sadness filled my spirit,
as my knocks go unanswered
upon my own windowpane.

A double minded man *is* unstable in all his ways. James 1:8

Truth stands the test of time; lies are soon exposed. Proverbs 12:19, NLT

Hear this, I pray you, ye heads of the house…and princes of the house…that abhor judgment, and pervert all equity. Micah 3:9

You have evicted women from their homes and stripped their children of all their God-given rights. Up! Begone! This is no longer your land and home, for you have filled it with sin and ruined it completely. Micah 2:9, NLT

He that sweareth to *his own* hurt, and changeth not...nor taketh reward against the innocent. He that doeth these *things* shall never be moved. Psalm 15:4–5

Jesus Christ, the same yesterday, and to day, and for ever. Hebrews 13:8

Increasing Their Own Kill

He collapsed like a reed,
when she looked to him for help.
When leaned upon…
he splintered,
and attempted to stab her to death.

When she put her weight on him,
he gave way…
and her back was thrown out.
When she pleaded
for a song of love,
only lies poured from his mouth.

He plots conspiracies against her,
just as a lion stalks his prey.
He's skilled at devouring the innocent,
and seizing treasures along his way.

He is like a wild animal lurking in the reeds.
For *he is* a wild animal,
mounting his next victim of feed.

His mouth covers her nose and mouth,
as she struggles to stay on her feet.
But he's hell bent to satisfy his sadistic appetite,
opening wide his jaws to eat.

The Lord says,
"They eat up My people like bread."
How he would no longer hunger and thirst,
if the Bread Of Life,
he would allow himself fed!

Sandra Wilson

But like a wolf,
he tears her apart,
enjoying destroying her life for profit.
His target...her house and car...
for she wasn't smart to keep his name off of it.

He chooses his body
to become the hideout of demons,
a nest for filthy buzzards.
He allows his body to be engraved
with all kinds of snakes and lizards.

He uses magic veils, enchantments, charms
and spells to ensnare her like a bird.
"Why can't I break away from you?" she asks,
as he grins, not saying a word.

If she *turns* to Jesus for deliverance,
his grin will no longer be.
For God has a system to help her
make *the turn in her captivity*.

God will help her renounce
and break soul ties to him;
dissolving the spell of her former company,
placing a release between them.

God will tear her from his arms,
setting her free from her cage.
He will tear off the magic veils,
saving her from his witchcraft rage.

The power of the Holy Spirit
will cut every hunger that should not be.
Every overload...
every excess of darkness, so she can wisely see.

God has angels
whose only business is to catch thieves.
Into the house of the thief,
to feast on his wealth…
bring him to his knees.

To those who practice witchcraft,
a ravenous spirit will be released.
These spirits drink human blood,
and feed on flesh, piece by piece.

That's why the wicked lives are shortened,
God won't let them live.
Their enjoyment of causing hardships for others,
is increasing their own kill.

My enemies surround me like a herd of bulls; fierce bulls… have hemmed me in! Like roaring lions attacking their prey, they come at me with open mouths…My enemies surround me like a pack of dogs; an evil gang closes in on me. They have pierced my hands and feet. I can count every bone in my body. My enemies stare at me and gloat. Psalm 22:12–17, NLT

…they which creep into houses, and lead captive silly women laden with sins, led away with diver lusts,
II Timothy 3:6

And I saw an angel standing in the sun; and he cried with a loud voice, saying to all the fowls that fly in the midst of heaven, Come and gather yourselves together unto the supper of the great God; That they may eat the flesh of kings, and the flesh of captains, and the flesh of mighty men...and all the fowls were filled with their flesh. Revelations 19:17–18, 21

Blessed *be* the Lord, who hath not given us *as* a prey to their teeth. Psalm 124:6

God Is Not In Your Past, So Why Are You?

He said he wanted a divorce;
then he phoned and said,
"Please don't."

I was just getting my heart
to move in my future direction.
Now since he said that…
"it won't."

Once he got me to change my walk,
he deceitfully backed away.

Now I've returned to playing solo in my past,
while he moved to his future play.

He phones every two or three weeks,
evaluating if my longing for him remains.

I know I'm fighting for my survival here!
God help me break this captive cycle of pain!

God spoke, He's not in my past.
He's in my now and future.

On my wounds,
He allowed His band-aid,
after applying His healing suture.

Sandra Wilson

So once again,
I reach for the new with outstretched hands.
From my past I snatch away.

I repeat my good-byes to the old,
but to my future,
I request it to stay.

*(You tried the olive tree and no luck; you tried the fig tree and no luck; you tried the grapevine and no luck; so you settled for a thornbush. Your self-portrait was so low until even the thornbush felt the power to give you an ultimatum. And the thornbush replied, "If you truly want to make me your king, come and take shelter in my shade" (Judges 9:8–15, NLT).

…into the hand of them that afflict thee; which have said to thy soul, Bow down, that we may go over: and thou hast laid thy body as the ground, and as the street, to them that went over. Isaiah 51:23

For there are many unruly and vain talkers and deceivers… Titus 1:10

But that which beareth thorns and briers *is* rejected; Hebrews 6:8

The LORD *is* thy keeper: the LORD *is* thy shade upon thy right hand. Psalm 121:5

...forgetting those things which are behind, and reaching forth unto those things which are before. Philippians 3:13

God setteth the solitary in families: Psalm 68:6

In Righteousness Shall You Be Established

Get out of that bed!
Lift up your head,
dry your tear stained face!

Put on some clothes!
Then your socks and your shoes.
Don't forget to lace!

Take a walk outside and breathe in
God's life-sustaining gas of love.

Look around at creation
and what has been made
by Our Heavenly Father above.

God wants to converse with you as you walk,
for you never walk alone,
He's near.

He wants to minister to your soul,
removing what your tormentor
is using... *Your Fear.*

(So open your mind and understanding
to what God is now saying in your ear):

"In righteousness shall you be established.
You shall be far from oppression.

In righteousness shall you be established.
You shall be far from terrorism.

Your oppressors shall surely gather together,
but not by me.

Whosoever shall gather, shall fall,
for gathering against thee.

I have created the blacksmith,
who uses coal and fire to bring
forth an instrument of joy.

I have also created the waster,
whom those who oppress,
I can assign him to destroy.

No weapon formed against you shall prosper;
every tongue that rise against you in judgment,
you shall condemn.

So your abusive tormentors
are not getting away with their wicked acts,
performed against you at their whim.

This is the heritage of the servants of the Lord,
and their righteousness is of Me.

I AM the God of your salvation,
you *will* be vindicated and set free!"

By reason of the multitude of oppressions they make *the oppressed* to cry; they cry out by reason of the arm of the mighty. Job 35:9

The Lord *is* nigh unto them that are of a broken heart; Psalm 34:18

...the root of the righteous shall not be moved...The wicked are overthrown, and *are* not, but the house of the righteous shall stand. Proverbs 12:3,7

...and thou shalt be called by a new name, which the mouth of the Lord shall name...Thou shalt no more be termed Forsaken; neither shall thy land any more be termed Desolate...for the Lord delighted in thee, and thy land shall be married. Isaiah 62:2, 4

To Those Are Wicked

To those who are wicked,
and choose to be that way.
To those who refuse
The Jesus Way to obey.

Your wickedness and pride
have reached a climax.
God, watching daily,
has been viewing all the facts.

He will remember and visit your iniquity,
upon your head comes the curse.
He allowed you space to make the *turn*,
but instead your wickedness got worse.

God said He will touch all your evilness.
Not one thing will go amiss.
You will not get away with your cruelty,
for God does fully assess.

Again and again,
your guilt cries out,
for you're not ashamed of your sins.
God has prepared destroyers against you…
skilled in battle to win.

You were never in control…
and never will be.
God decides who rise and fall;
a truth you refuse to see.

Sandra Wilson

For Satan has you as his deceived captive,
thinking through him you live.
But his LIVE is turned backwards,
all you'll ever get from him is EVIL.

If you do not repent,
cruel men have been appointed,
each carrying a battle club in his hand.
The angel of the Lord has been sent forth to smote…
destroyer angels from God's band.

An army has been brought,
you will be terrorized and plundered.
Now it's your season to cry, fret about,
flounder and wonder.

God has his own special hunters and fishers,
turn from being an enemy against God!
You think you've covered your steps;
but the Father knows every where your feet has trod.

Your camp will become your enemy,
and begin to deal treacherously with you.
You will drink from the same cup of terror;
but double…for what you put others through.

…the great is fallen, is fallen, and is become the habitation of devils, and the hold of every foul spirit, and a cage of every unclean and hateful bird. Revelation 18:2

And I (Jesus) gave…space to repent…Revelation 2:21

Turn In Your Captivity!

...I will put you on trial. I will be a ready witness against all sorcerers and adulterers and liars...for these people do not fear me," says the Lord Almighty. Malachi 3:5, NLT

Behold I will send for many fishers, saith the Lord, and they shall fish them; and after will I send for many hunters, and they shall hunt them from every mountain, and from every hill, and out of the holes of the rocks. For mine eyes *are* upon all their ways: they are not hid from my face, neither is their iniquity hid from mine eye. Jeremiah 16:16–17

...Thus saith the Lord; Such *as are* for death, to death; and such *as are* for the sword, to the sword; and such *as are* for the famine, to the famine; and such *as are* for the captivity, to the captivity. Jeremiah 15:2

I Knew Pain

When I was lonely,
and that feeling brought so much pain,
I thought about going back
to my old ways,
and even my old abusive man.

But instead I cried myself to sleep,
as I asked Jesus to hold me tight.
I meditated on God's Word,
because I knew this choice was right.

I knew it was good
to continue in hope for a godly mate.
I knew it was good
for impatience to be replaced by wait.

I knew it was good
to guard against Satan,
who comes stealing.

I knew all these things,
but still had to force my flesh
to be willing.

I knew I could not fight
flesh on my own.
But it was through Christ Jesus
my own will was made strong.

Strong enough to defend God's Word,
and to take a stand.
Strong enough to confront the pain,
and take it like a wo-man.

I learned from my fight with flesh,
I had a fear of pain.
Listening to the lies of the devil,
I believed it could drive me insane.

So away from hurt I used to run,
no matter what the cost.
This was causing my liberty
and self-control to be lost.

I knew it was wrong
to be angry so quickly.
I knew deep inside
my feelings were too prickly.

I knew it was wrong
to not listen…to not obey.
I knew I shouldn't always
try to get things done my way.

But through the power of the Word,
I learned to submit to God's will.
When pain rises up,
I simply say, "Peace be still."

Jesus is my rod and staff,
and will always comfort me.
His life He freely gave,
so from flesh I'm made free.

I'm glad I didn't listen
to what the devil had to say.
I stood strong in my faith,
and did it The Jesus Way.

I thank God that His Word
brings a *turn* around.
From the old life I refrain,
because a joyous new life I've found.

Facing the pain,
holding Jesus' hand,
I've learned hurt will not always last.
Now I stare pain in the face
and tell it, "This too shall pass!"

At least I can take comfort in this: Despite the pain, I have not denied the words of the Holy One. Job 6:10, NLT

And God shall wipe away all tears from their eyes; and there shall be no more death, neither sorrow, nor crying, neither shall there be any more pain: for the former things are passed away. Revelation 21:4

Suicide Prevention

Did you say you want to end it all
because you can not handle the pains of life?
Make a choice to think only on things
godly and spiritually right.

Taking your life is not of God.
Satan has been attacking you…
and attacking you mighty hard.

He doesn't want you
in God's order and grace.
He causes failure and condemnation,
then laughs right in your face.

Satan is a liar and a deceiver too.
He doesn't want you to follow Jesus,
because then you'll learn the truth.

You have the power to bind Satan
and cause him to flee from you.
This power comes from Jesus Christ,
whom you work through.

Open your mouth and know
you have the words of command.
"In the name of Jesus,
the blood of Jesus,"
is how you take your stand.

See Satan wants your mouth shut,
holding tight to fears and cares.
But Jesus Christ defeated him,
so now don't you dare!

You can be, and have the right to be,
delivered from Satanic influence.
So speak and believe in the name of Jesus;
He's your paid in full life insurance.

Know you fight not against flesh and blood,
but Satanic principalities.
Breaking from toxic people
and bad habits have to become your reality.

The bible says we have not,
because we ask not,
so don't let this be your fate.
Ask God to give you His hedge of protection
and a way of escape.

Ask Him to be a lamp unto your feet
and a light unto your path.
Know what you do for Christ
is the only thing that will last.

Ask God for godly wisdom,
and development of godly skills.
He will show you what to do,
in order to stay within His will

Your body is the temple of God,
in which you have no right to end.
You're mighty, unique,
and precious in God's sight,
and Jesus' dearest friend.

Ask Jesus to be your comfort,
He will make your pain not hurt so bad.
You will be amazed to awake
from the best sleep you ever had.

Just wrap your arms around yourself,
and squeeze real tight.
That's just the love of Jesus
saying, *"Everything is going to be alright."*

He that is our God *is* the God of salvation; and unto GOD the Lord *belong* the issues from death. Psalm 68:20

For I have no pleasure in the death of him that dieth, saith the Lord God: wherefore turn *yourselves*, and live ye. Ezekiel 18:32

And in the face of death, wickedness will certainly not rescue those who practice it. Ecclesiastes 8:8, NLT

...I (Jesus) am come that they might have life, and that they might have it more abundantly. John 10:10

Lemonade or Gatorade?

Have you heard the saying,
when life throws you lemons,
make Lemonade?

Well there are some people
whose Lemonade tastes a little funny,
in fact, it taste more like Gatorade.

Did they use the correct ingredients?
Forgiveness mixed with sweetness
stirred together till well-blended.

Or did they look at the lemons
that were thrown to them,
and get highly offended?

Did they just measure in some hate
mixed with a dash of bitterness,
thinking it tasted just fine?

I know I don't want
any of their concoction,
poured into any vessel of mine!

Lemonade or Gatorade?
Do you have time
to change your recipe?

Change it on today,
because tomorrow
is not promised to thee.

…I (God) would not that ye should have fellowship with devils. Ye cannot drink the cup of the Lord, and the cup of devils: ye cannot be partakers of the Lord's table, and of the table of devils. I Corinthians 10:20–21

That every one of you should know how to possess his vessel in sanctification and honour; I Thessalonians 4:4

"Women, Take Care Of Your Temple"

As women, we have to take care of ourselves.
No one else can do it for us.
Don't feel you cannot accomplish this goal,
remember in God we trust.

Our bodies are the temple of God,
and in our bodies His Spirit dwells.
Whatever we do behind closed doors,
out in the open it will eventually tell.

Could it be we're not taking care of ourselves
because we do not have the skill?
The skills of self-love, self-protection,
and self-preservation are definitely within God's will.

Or maybe you were not aware
the need for skill exist.
Not doing things The Jesus Way,
are you willing to take that risk?

The risk of not seeing God's purpose
for your life fulfilled.
The suffering of your spirit
from not being within God's will.

The risk of bodily injury, diseases, and destruct.
The risk of allowing the devil
in your bodily temple to run amuck.

The devil can bring hypertension, diabetes,
glaucoma, and stroke.
Cancer, arthritis, and coronary artery disease
are no joke.

But the Good News is
sickness is not of God.
To the bible for the wisdom of skill
is where our feet should trod.

So vow to take better care of yourself,
and do it The Jesus Way.
Don't start on tomorrow or a month from now,
but vow to start today.

*(Those who are involved in abusive relationships have poorer health and a lower quality of life than individuals who are not in such relationships. For example, women who experience Intimate Partner Violence (IPV) are much more likely to suffer from various injuries (e.g., head and facial trauma) and are also at greater risk for experiencing chronic pain, arthritis, migraines, and kidney disease. In addition, women involved in abusive relationships are at increased risk for developing depression, anxiety, post-traumatic stress disorder, and low self-esteem.)

By the great force *of my disease* is my garment changed: it bindeth me about as the collar of my coat. Job 30:18

When Jesus heard *that*, he said, *This sickness is not unto death...*
John 11:4

I have seen what they do, but I will heal them anyway! I will lead them and comfort those who mourn. Isaiah 57:18–19, NLT

Stop Sacrificing Yourself, Yourself

Are you sacrificing yourself
out of your own obedience?

Well stop sacrificing yourself,
yourself!

God doesn't want us to do this
type of sacrificing.

This we do out of
what our own flesh have felt.

Obey the Word and that in itself
is the self-sacrifice.

Speak as Jesus,
"Not My will, but Your will Father,"
just before He gave His life.

Sacrifice without obedience
to God is dead.

Obedience is better than sacrifice,
in the bible is what I read.

So we should not blindly give ourselves to man.
To God submit your total surrender.

Sandra Wilson

God will love us unconditionally,
whereas man may become our brute offender.

We say to man,
"See my good deeds.
I sacrificed to give to you. Now you owe me!"

But man doesn't see our sacrifice.
He sees only our pride that be.

It's not about us
and what we've done.
It's just not a matter of care.

Jesus Christ paid the price by sacrificing His life.
Did the cross on our backs we bear?

You can not approach the throne of God
unless you bring Jesus Christ before you.

His blood and His name purifies your way.
So to thy own self be true.

Are you sacrificing yourself
out of your own obedience?

Well stop sacrificing yourself,
yourself!

The fool foldeth his hands together, and eateth his own flesh.
Ecclesiastes 4:5

And have no root in themselves, and so endure but for a time: Mark 4:17

But be ye doers of the word, and not hearers only, deceiving your own selves. James 1:22

…present your bodies a living sacrifice, holy, acceptable unto God, which is your reasonable service. Romans 12:1

These things I (Jesus) speak in the world, that they might have my joy fulfilled in themselves. John 17:13

Chapter 2.

Jesus Loves and Cares For You

(He's Just That Way!)

God so loved the world that He gave His only begotten Son; and Jesus loved us so until He volunteered to become the mediator for the sake of mankind. *Turn In Your Captivity, Ending Abuse in Marriages and Relationships The Jesus Way* proclaims with a shout, "Jesus is the Way, the Truth, and the Life!" He loves and cares for us and does not want us to grieve or anyone to cause us grief. Jesus said, *I will love him, and will manifest myself to him* (John 14:21). Who shall separate us from the love of Christ?

Jesus left many examples of His love while here on earth, and now in heaven, His deep love and care for us continues! Although Jesus came from glory, there was nothing beautiful or majestic about His appearance, nothing to attract us to Him (Isaiah 53:2). But through His lack, He gave us beauty for our ashes. Although royalty, He became a carpenter that we would receive the wealth of the world. Jesus never sinned, but He died for sinners that we might become the righteousness of God. He was wounded that we might have peace. He was whipped and we were healed! Jesus willingly carried heavy burdens so that our cross would be easy and light. He took our shame upon Himself that we would become fearless and have root in ourselves. Even though He became overwhelmed to the point where He sweated blood, Jesus pressed toward the mark and continued out of love for us...enduring for our sakes. He allowed Himself to be violated so we could have our rights and privileges upheld. He became a servant that by His service of salvation, He could make us kings and queens, princes and princesses, priests and priestesses.

Jesus said, *If you hear me calling and open the door (your heart), I will come in, and we will share a meal as friends* (Revelation 3:20, NLT). Satan pretends to be the friend of many to their faces, but when in the presence of God, he's judging, accusing and condemning them. But Jesus, our friend and redeemer, stood in the gap for our defense, and is now in heaven interceding on our behalf. He said; *Do not think that I will accuse you to the Father* (John 5:45). *The Son of man is not come to destroy men's lives, but to save them* (Luke 9:56). He is a friend that sticks closer than any brother, even to His own hurt. At His hour of betrayal and suffering, Jesus said, *I have told you that I am he: if therefore ye seek me, let these go their way* (John 18:8). For our sakes, Jesus chose not to exercise His power to deliver Himself. The band of men who came to take Jesus went backward and fell to the ground, just from His answering, *I am he* (John 18:3–6). He showed His love for us when He asked God to send a Comforter, One who would continue to give us love and guidance. As a perfect friend, Jesus does not change, run from us, make Himself a stranger, or show indifference, but when we call upon Him, He answers. When we seek Him, He avails Himself. When we knock, He opens the door and warmly invites us in.

Jesus fought Satan and all evil, giving us authority and power over them; whereby, evil is casted into outer darkness at our command. He took the keys of hell and death from Satan, returning to us the keys to the Kingdom of Heaven and right standing with God. He loved us so until He shut the gates of hell and made death just a transition into eternal life. Salvation is available to all mankind, Jews and Gentiles alike. All can be children of God...Sons and Daughters...heirs to the kingdom. Whom the Lord makes free is free indeed!

Jesus restored to us *Life*; not only eternal life in heaven, but life here in the land of the living. Yes, we can be confident that we will see the Lord's goodness, because Jesus said, *behold, I send the promise of my Father upon you* (Luke 24:49). All that God rewarded Jesus, He divided with the righteous. But the greatest show of love was the giving of

His life. Jesus freely gave up the ghost Himself, no man took His life. Then He went to the prison of hell preaching to those spirits who lived on earth before the flood, but disobeyed God. Jesus allowed them a chance to live according to God in the spirit. He wants us to have eternal life, and is gone to prepare a place, and will return to be joined unto us. Jesus awaits, anticipating us eating with Him in Paradise. He is lovingly preparing a great feast for us! Great rewards! He is our Savior! Our big brother! And like a big brother's love, Jesus takes care of us!

This Is The Man

"Guilty!" they shouted.
"He must die!"
Then spit in His face,
and hit Him with their fists.

This is the Man
who was betrayed with a kiss.

Some slapped Him, saying,
"Prophesy to us,
who hit You that time?"

This is the Man
who turned water into wine.

The next day
He was bound and taken to Pilate.

This is the Man
who was abused and violated.

He was flogged,
then given to the soldiers
to crucify.

This is the Man
who volunteered
for our sins to die.

Sandra Wilson

They stripped Him,
dressing Him in a purple robe,
placing a crown of
thorns on His head.

This is the Man
who we now have redemption,
because of His blood that was shed.

A stick in His right hand as a scepter;
they mocked,
"Hail! King of the Jews!"

This is the Man
who stood on the mount
preaching and teaching
the Good News.

They spit on Him,
grabbed the stick,
beating Him on the head with it.

This is the Man
who delivered the boy possessed
with demonic fits.

Finally tired of mocking,
they took off the robe
putting His clothes on again.

This is the Man
who endured the sufferings,
and His own life did not defend.

Led away to be crucified,
He refused wine
mixed with bitter gall.

This is the Man
who was innocent of sin,
but for us was taking the fall.

Nailed to the cross,
soldiers gambled for His clothes
by throwing dice.

This is the Man
who was denied three times
before the rooster crowed twice.

It was nine o'clock
as they sat around;
a signboard was fastened
above His head.

This is the Man
who hung beneath the sign,
The King Of The Jews,
is how it read.

Two criminals were crucified with Him,
their crosses on either side.

This is the Man
who foretold of His death,
even before He died.

The people shouted,
"If you're the Son of God,
save yourself. Come down
from the cross!"

This is the Man
who the people did not know
was redeeming their souls
from being lost.

Sandra Wilson

At noon, darkness for three hours
across the whole land fell.

This is the Man
who at 3 o'clock,
called out with a loud yell,

"My God, My God,
why hast Thou forsaken Me?"

This is the Man
who for you and me
suffered tremendously.

A sponge with vinegar
held on a stick was offered
so He could drink.

This is the Man
with more wealth
than the bystanders could ever think.

"Let's see whether Elijah
will come to save Him,"
the rest of the bystanders said.

This is the Man
who gave up His Spirit,
allowing His body to be dead.

The curtain in the Temple
was torn in two,
the earth shook,
and tombs opened wide.

After the Man's resurrection,
many raised from the dead,
appeared in Jerusalem very much alive.

The roman officers and soldiers
at the crucifixion, said,
"Truly this was the Son of God!"

This is the Man,
Jesus Christ, Who is, Who always was,
and Who is still to come,
affecting a change in people's hearts.

Who, being in the form of God, thought it not robbery to be equal with God: But made himself of no reputation, and took upon him the form of a servant, and was made in the likeness of men: And being found in fashion as a man, he humbled himself, and became obedient unto death, even the death of the cross. Wherefore God also hath highly exalted him, and given him a name which is above every name: That at the name of Jesus every knee should bow, of *things* in heaven, and *things* in earth, and *things* under the earth; And *that* every tongue should confess that Jesus Christ *is* Lord, to the glory of God the Father. Philippians 2:6–11

But now is Christ risen from the dead, *and* become the first fruits of them that slept. For since by man *came* death, by man *came* also the resurrection of the dead. For as in Adam all die, even so in Christ shall all be made alive. I Corinthians 15:20–22

A Man Named Jesus Christ

I was rescued from being aborted
by a Man named Jesus Christ.
He fought the violent mob to get to me,
and I noticed His many stripes.

He took me home to raise as His own.
I started with a baby crawl.
He fed me the milk of His Word,
and placed a pillow where I might fall.

He held me in His arms of protection,
and comforted me when I cried.
He understood I was scared,
because without Him, I would've died.

He changed me when I made mistakes,
even though I made them over
and over again.
He didn't mind washing
and cleaning me up,
securing me with a safety pin.

Then I started walking for Jesus.
He held my hand as I went.
He strengthened my legs with His exercises,
'cause they were pretty bent.

He guided my way as I walked to Him.
Many times I would fall.
He would help me up, dust me off,
and say, *"Try again, that's all."*

Along the way I broke many things,
but He would say, *"That's okay."*
He encouraged me to stay inside
and not go out to play.

Jesus went with me on my first day
at the School of Hard Knocks.
He protected me from bullies
that were hitting me with rocks.

One day when I didn't come home,
but went and played in the park,
He whipped me for my disobedience,
but it didn't leave a mark.

Then I started running for Jesus.
I excelled in my studies too.
I passed all my tests. I did my best,
and Jesus said, *"Good for you!"*

He hugged me on my day of graduation,
and gave me a gift of the Spirit.
I felt real proud, as Jesus said out loud,
"Now all your struggles have merit."

He helped me dress for graduation,
as I put on the whole armor of God.
He rode with me to the ceremony,
and nudged me as I nod.

Jesus beamed as I stood on the stage,
giving my graduation speech.
That's when it dawned on me,
my gift was the gift to teach.

I took a full time job after graduation,
babysitting others in Jesus' care.
The work was hard, but the pay was good.
It made me a billionaire.

Invitations are sent to only the Righteous.
The church is full and well-adorned.
I'm standing in my wedding dress,
awaiting the sound of Gabriel's horn.

My bridegroom is coming,
I can see Him way afar.
We will marry 'cause my dress
is pure white, without a spot or mar.

We will take the flight to heaven,
and those invited will come along.
We're going to a prepared place
where there's no hurt and no wrong.

…in the day thou wast born thy navel was not cut, neither was thou washed in water to supple *thee*; thou wast not salted at all, not swaddled at all. None eye pitied thee to do any of these unto thee, to have compassion upon thee; but thou wast cast out in the open field, to the lothing of thy person, in the day that thou wast born. And when I (God) passed by thee, and saw thee polluted in thine own blood, I said unto thee *when thou wast* in thy blood, Live; yea, I said unto thee *when thou wast* in thy blood, Live. Ezekiel 16:4–6

God sent forth his Son (Jesus Christ)…To redeem them that were under the law. That we might receive the adoption of Sons (Daughters). Galatians 4:4–5

You (Lord) will keep guiding me with your counsel, leading me to a glorious destiny. Psalm 73:24, NLT

God's Captivity Training

There are three ways of being in captivity:
You bring it on yourself
Others cause it to come
God permits it as a demonstration of faith.

For you, God has not chosen the first two,
but through your misery He teaches you,
how your captivity to annihilate.

The resulting demise of the first two
is to destroy, steal, and kill.

But God's permitted captivity
promotes oppressive wounds
to heal.

God doesn't want anyone oppressed.
But since you're in captivity…
He uses captivity to bring you out.

Since you have trouble,
He uses trouble to train you
what faith in Him is about.

We are children of God…
children of the resurrection;
God trains His children in the way to go.

He established the rod,
and even spoke its use
to earthly parents on their children to bestow.

Foolishness is bound in the heart of a child;
but the rod of correction drives it far from him.

The rod is not meant as a provocation of anger.
God is not using it on us at His whim.

Well why does He do it?
To whom does He do it?
At what time does He know to do it?

We all need to comprehend the workings of God.
I pray your understanding as I take you through it.

(The bible says,
The blueness of a wound cleanses away evil:
so do stripes the inward parts of the belly.)

God does not wound;
He just adds blueness to our wounds
that already exist.

Wounds are no fault of God;
but of Satan, others and ourselves,
who think, speak and act amiss.

They came as a result
of our own self-afflictions,
and influences of those
operating in evil.

The blueness and stripes,
impart God's healing.
Because He doesn't want His children
weak and feeble.

What are the blueness and stripes
God uses to cleanse us,
on our outsides
and in our inward parts?

It's the fire He permits to come upon us,
so accept the burn;
don't choose your wounds to be fire retard.

As in nature, the fire that can kill,
also helps to sustain.

Allow it to do its cleansing;
when upon you begins the flame.

The way to walk you will see
as your path is cleared by God's fire.

You will know the way
and see your enemies,
as you walk the way God requires.

In the world you shall have tribulations,
but it's the world Jesus
has already victoriously overcome.

He prayed to God,
*"Not that Thou should take them out of the world
but that Thou should keep them from the evil."*
For you see, it's evil, not trouble,
we should shun.

God's permitted captivity
are necessary for you
to get to your place of power.

Not all troubles are bad;
some make you glad they were had.
You're transformed into a stronger tower.

Before antidote,
what was used on a snake bite?
Fire.

The wound received a chaser insult,
killing toxins, before its victim expires.

Abuse to oneself and others,
inflict external and inner wounds,
you may or may not see.

God bruises these wounds
to foster their healing,
so the woundings will no longer be.

Wounded tissue can become dark and dead;
the surgeon cuts it away to sustain life.

When our gangrenous wounds
are trying to kill us,
God, the Surgeon,
pulls out His expert cutting device.

God uses His stripes to cleanse our inner wounds,
because its drainage has
clogged our inward parts.

As the roto-rooter man,
God works the rod in His hand,
opening deep belly wounds that are hard.

He wants the Bread of Life
He feeds us to flow freely,
not stop at our stomach's entrance in defeat.

God says,
*"Open wide your mouth and eat what I give you.
You're not a glutton if you feast
on what I give you to eat."*

Welcome God's rod
to clear your inward woundings,
so your belly's rivers of living waters
can flow free.

Command it to flow to all areas of your scars,
for it carries God's powers of victory.

Stand confident in God's correction,
instead of your chest…
stick out your belly!

For He loves you
regardless of your open wounds
being infected and smelly.

Your mind and body
will initially fight the discomfort.
Yes, bruising hurts and stripes do cause a sting.

But surrender to God's rod,
as you learn the skill
of allowing yourself to be godly clean.

God whips to cause the blueness and stripes
while there is still hope for your survival.

He's helping you to be well enough...
in your right mind enough...to see clear enough...
to rightly hear enough,
before the terminal toxins make their arrival.

Because some wounds,
can become so infected
until death is too much to the tissues.

We can wait too late;
we saw the pus draining,
but refused to address this issue.

God whips out of love to save our lives;
but we do not understand,
or choose to take offense.

We leave our place of divine training,
divine cleansing, and divine purpose.
God allows us to freely choose, so hence...

We're turned over to a reprobate mind,
because God's bruising and stripes
only make us mad and madder.

God says, *"I did not choose this grief for you;
this evil captivity...this demise,"*
as the heart of God becomes sad and sadder.

Who hath woe? who hath sorrow? who hath contentions?
who hath babbling? who hath wounds without cause?...
Proverbs 23:29

Sandra Wilson

But by means of their suffering, he (God) rescues those who suffer. For he gets their attention through adversity. Job 36:15, NLT

The blueness of a wound cleanseth away evil: so do stripes the inward parts of the belly. Proverbs 20:30

Good Watchman Story

"Honey, where are you going dressed like that?"
asked Kirk,
as his wife tried to slip pass him and out the door.

"I told you I was going out with the girls.
It's ladies' night out.
So don't be scrutinizing and asking me what for."

Linda looks down at her dress,
"What's wrong with this?
Yes, I'm going to a club."

"Well," said Kirk, "It looks like you're selling yourself…
like you're advertising…I'm available for love.

Clubbing is mainly for the single's scene.
I'm saying this as a warning.
I'm not trying to be controlling or mean.

You're a married woman,
your girlfriends are not.
They're going hoping to meet a man…
their Sir Lancelot."

"No, we already talked about that.
This is a night out for ourselves.
If a man try and break us up,
we'll tell him to go somewhere else."

"As your watchman, I'm just warning you
what God has placed in my spirit.
You need to change your company,
and I hope you will hear it."

"I'll be okay I promise,
and I won't do nothing wrong.
I already know I have my Sir Lancelot
waiting for me at home."

Kirk shrugged his shoulders
as he watched Linda leave.
He said a prayer of protection
because his spirit man was grieved.

At the club, sure enough, Linda mostly sat alone.
Her girlfriends were dancing,
exchanging phone numbers, and busy staying gone.

Guys were coming as swarms
around Linda at her solitary table,
asking for a dance and her phone number,
which she told them she was not able.

Some of the guys got angry, saying,
"Oh you're just a tease.
Why did you come dressed like that
if you're not aiming to please?"

Her girlfriends said,
"Go on, Kirk will never know."
But Linda held her head in shame,
as her condemnation begins to show.

"Where did Linda go?"
her girlfriends asked,
as they finally came to sit down.

They searched the club,
the front and the back…
but Linda could not be found.

She snuggles under her Sir Lancelot
as he beamingly drives her home.
Kirk had rushed to pick her up,
when from the club, Linda phoned.

Son of man, I have made thee a watchman unto the house…therefore hear the word at my mouth, and give them warning from me. Ezekiel 3:17

Unfailing love and faithfulness protect the king; his throne is made secure through love. Proverbs 20:28, NLT

…a prudent wife *is* from the LORD. Proverbs 19:14

Mercy and truth are met together; righteousness and peace have kissed each *other*. Psalm 85:10

Who Knows...But Jesus?

As I sat in the emergency room,
I examined the many faces there.
Who knows of their many problems?
Who knows of their many cares?

I observed the faces to catch a glimpse
of what made them come.
Some appeared frightened,
as if at any moment,
they may jump up and run.

Some appeared to be in pain,
as if they could not take it any more.
Others appeared to have no concerns,
as they tilted their heads, slept, and snored.

Some came limping in,
as others walked in slow.
Some faces showed aggravation,
as their waiting time continued to grow.

I may not know what they're dealing with,
but Jesus Christ certainly does.
I prayed a silent prayer God
would shower them with His love.

I prayed God would lighten the loads
and burdens that were there.
And the people would learn,
with God, their troubles to share.

We're to bring our burdens to Jesus Christ,
and leave them there.
Isn't it wonderful we have a Savior
who shows His love and care?

Jesus is our Way Maker,
our present help in times of trouble.
It's our job to seek His face,
so our problems don't increase and double.

People can never predict when hard times might come. Like fish in a net or birds in a snare, people are often caught by sudden tragedy...When you dig a well, you may fall in. When you demolish an old wall, you could be bitten by a snake. When you work in a quarry, stones might fall and crush you! When you chop wood, there is danger with each stroke of your axe! Such are the risks of life. Ecclesiastes 9:12; 10:8–9, NLT

They (the innocent) will survive through hard times; even in famine they will have more than enough. Psalm 37:19, NLT

The righteous cry, and the LORD heareth, and delivereth them out of all their troubles. Psalm 34:17

With Empathy

With empathy, I bring these words
to help you in your time of need.

Your situation is very painful now,
and I know your heart grieves.

I'm praying God
will be your sustaining grace.

For abuse is a difficult circumstance
for anyone to face.

Know God's promises will make it easier,
as each day goes by.

Know the shoulder of Jesus is available,
if you ever need to cry.

Know Jesus loves you
and cares about how you're treated.
He's just a prayer call away.

Know if you're seeking deliverance,
through Jesus there's victory,
all you have to do is obey.

Remember them that are in bonds, as bound with them; and them which suffer adversity, as being yourselves also in the body. Hebrews 13:3

Not because I desire a gift: but I desire fruit that may abound to your account. Philippians 4:17

If your gift is to encourage others, do it! Romans 12:8, NLT

Rather Than The Other

Being with an abusive man
has caused me stress and pain.

But Jesus Christ is my Savior
and He took away my shame.

That is why I chose Christ,
rather than the other.

I was feeling bad
and looking older than my mother.

I chose the One who gives me
wisdom and knowledge,

rather than the one
who could make me an alcoholic.

The One who helps me to spiritually grow,

rather than the one
who enjoys the reapings,
but never seems to sow.

The One who sets me free,

rather than the one
who has women three.

The One who knows the shape I'm in,

rather than the one
who I visit in the State Pen.

The One who gives me joy and hope,

rather than the one
who caused my bankruptcy,
buying him that boat.

The One who makes me promises
He always keeps,

rather than the one
who I haven't seen in about a week.

The One who shows me
how to walk in victory,

rather than the one
who is always up to some trickery.

The One who says yes,

rather than the one who says no.

The One who says fast,

rather than the one who says slow.

These are the reasons
why I chose Jesus Christ.

Chosing the other
is just too high a price.

Plus with him
I will live a captive, oppressed life.

But now, after that ye have known God, or rather are known of God, how turn ye again to the weak and beggarly elements, whereunto ye desire again to be in bondage? Galatians 4:9

But I beseech *you* the rather to do this…Hebrews 13:19

…exercise thyself *rather* unto godliness…godliness is profitable unto all things, having promise of the life that now is, and of that which is to come. I Timothy 4:7–8

Art thou called *being* a servant? care not for it: but if thou mayest be made free, use *it* rather. I Corinthians 7:21

Your Self-Worth

To control you for whatever reason,
some people will try to lower your self-esteem.
But don't buy into their schemes,
out of the mouth of God,
you're kings and queens!

Who knows best who and what you are,
than your Creator.
You're made in God's image.
You're His impersonator.

What is the worth
God placed upon you?
You'll have a renewed spirit…
a renewed mind…and a renewed view,
when the truths of God get through.

You're a child of the Lord God…
a child of the resurrection…
a child of light.
And because you're
a child of the Most High,
you should stand
in the God-given beauty of your might.

God's glory is in your body.
What is His glory?…His breath.
To you, of Himself, He gave.
As the heaven and stars,
you're the light of the world,
because you're brilliantly made.

God delights in you!
The very hairs on your head are numbered,
and there shall not a hair perish.
He looks from heaven
upon all the inhabitants of the earth,
for each day, you, in His arms,
He cherish.

You're God's masterpiece…
a kind of first fruit of His creatures.
So take the center stage!
You're the headline…the main feature!

God loves you so,
He refuses to let you go;
re-establishing your fellowship
with Him through Jesus Christ.
For you're valuable!
God brought you with a price!
You're not some inexpensive,
worthless merchandise.

God is mighty and despises no one.
It's the sin He hates, not the sinner.
So knock Satan out…pin him down for the count.
It's your hand that'll be raised as the winner!

God calls you by name.
You're chosen to receive The Good News!
Because of the Redeemer of your life,
you're as entitled to salvation as the Jews.

Jesus said, *"You have not chosen me,*
I have chosen you;
so go, bring forth fruit
and let your fruit remain.

*And you may have
whatsoever you shall ask of the Father
in My name."*

God, as a proud Father,
always points to us
as examples of the incredible wealth of His favor.
He wants the world to *see you*,
not what you've been through.
So self-worth and value,
you need to savor.

To acquire wisdom is to love oneself.
Jesus said, *"Don't sacrifice yourself,
just be merciful."*
Know you're the salt of the earth,
have salt in yourself.
Salt is good…be a whole spoon full.

The eyes of the Lord run to and fro,
showing Himself strong for those
whose hearts are perfect toward Him.
You have dominion over the works of your hands,
all things under your feet.
So the spirit of low self-esteem, you condemn!

Don't allow yourself to be pushed around,
God maintains your rights and cause.
He put you in charge of things He made,
giving you authority and use of His spiritual laws.

You're the first and not the last,
above and not beneath,
a lender and not a borrower.
Blessed going out and blessed coming in,
your hands to prosper,
and more than a conqueror.

Jesus said, *"I will not leave you comfortless;*
I will come to you.
No man is able to pluck you out of God's hand."
You are a Victor, not a victim,
as will be manifested;
as you go through the process to mend...
to heal...and to understand.

If you still feel low,
do you place more of your love onto others,
than you do for yourself and God?
If you refuse to take up your cross
and follow Jesus,
the truth is your worthiness *is* marred.

But God said,
"I have seen what they do,
and I will heal them anyway."
So love God back!
Low self-worth you attack!
You are what God says!

But by the grace of God I am what I am: and his grace which *was bestowed* upon me was not in vain...I Corinthians 15:10

Therefore let no man glory in men. For all things are your's: Whether...the world, or life, or death, or things present, or things to come: all are yours: And ye are Christ's; and Christ *is* God's. I Corinthians 3:21–23

A little one shall become a thousand, and a small one a strong nation: I the Lord will hasten it in his time. Isaiah 60:22

Today Is The Day

Today is the day to be saved.
No wait! I will do it on tomorrow.
For today, I cannot concentrate.
For today, I'm consumed with sorrow.

I have too many problems
and circumstances on my mind.
I will eventually give my life to God,
but on some other time.

No wait! God promises comfort
to him with sorrow in his life.
I must repent of my sinful ways
and start putting away my strife.

Weeping will only endure for a night
when I give my life to Christ.
I'm going to stop procrastinating
and allowing myself to think twice.

Even though I've always been like this,
it's time to change my ways.
I know God does not procrastinate;
He does just what He says.

Jesus understands sorrow,
for He went through sorrow too.
The sufferings He endured is in the bible,
as it is told to you.

Sandra Wilson

When Jesus returns, in His kingdom,
sorrow will exist no more.
Today is the day to be saved!
From this moment,
Jesus Christ is whom I'm living for.

He that believeth and is baptized shall be saved…Mark 16:16

Dear Jesus, I believe that You died for me and rose again on the third day. I confess I am a sinner. I need Your love and forgiveness. Come into my heart. Forgive my sins. I receive Your eternal life. Confirm Your love by giving me peace, joy and supernatural love for others. Amen.

Bless the LORD, O my soul, and forget not all his benefits: Who forgiveth all thine iniquities; who healeth all thy diseases; Who redeemeth thy life from destruction; who crowneth thee with lovingkindness and tender mercies; Who satisfieth thy mouth with *good things; so that* thy youth is renewed like the eagle's. Psalm 103:2–5

But if I (Jesus) with the finger of God cast out devils, no doubt the kingdom of God is come upon you. Luke 11:20

*(God has revealed unto me a revelation concerning His benefits which are bestowed upon us through Christ Jesus when we are saved. **These benefits attack, destroy at the root, and cast out each of the anti-christ 666.**)

1. Your sins are touched	1. all	1. forgiven
2. Your diseases are touched	2. all	2. healed
3. Your life is touched	3. from destruction	3. redeemed
4. Your head is touched	4. with loving-kindness and tender mercies	4. crowned
5. Your mouth is touched	5. with good things	5. satisfied
6. Your youth is touched	6. like the eagle's	6. renewed

Goodness!

Isn't it a freeing revelation to know
salvation is not based on our goodness?

God crowned me with his tender mercies
and His loving-kindness.

I didn't have to earn God's love,
because my Heavenly Father accepted me.

He told me to come just as I am,
and used Jesus' blood to make me free.

Thank God for the liberty!

…"Only God is good…" Matthew 19:17, NLT

He saved us, not because of the good things we did, but because of his mercy…He generously poured out the Spirit upon us because of what Jesus Christ our Savior did. Titus 3:5–6, NLT

Oh that men would praise the Lord for his goodness, and for his wonderful works to the children of men! Psalm 107:15

Praise the Lord!

Praise the Lord, I tell myself!
With my whole heart,
I will praise His holy name.

Praise the Lord, I tell myself!
I will never forget the good things
He allows on me to rain.

The Lord is slow to anger
and full of unfailing love.

For His mercy is as great
as the height of the heavens above.

He will not constantly accuse us,
nor remain angry forever.

Punishing and dealing with us
as we deserve is not His endeavor.

Tenderness and compassion
to those who obey Him
is what the Lord entrusts.

For He understands how weak we are.
He knows we're only dust.

His salvation extends to the
children's children of those
who are faithful to His covenant!

Sandra Wilson

His salvation extends to the
children's children of those
who obey His commandments!

Praise the Lord, I tell myself!

Great is his (the Lord's) faithfulness; his mercies begin afresh each day. Lamentations 3:23, NLT

...that they might be unto me (the Lord) for a people, and for a name, and for a praise, and for a glory: Jeremiah 13:11

The Prayer

The bible says with your own mouth
you will confess your own salvation;
and with your heart you will believe.

So speak for yourself,
for it is God, not man,
whom you have to please.

PRAYER:

"O God, I'm sorry
I have not done your will as I should.
I repent of that and more.

I ask you for the *turn in my captivity*,
and my place of dominion to restore.

I renounce in my life
every controlling witch, sorcerer,
evil manipulator, and voodoo.

Get out of my life!
You do not belong to me,
and I do not belong to you!

Lord, teach me how to break
controlling wills
that attempt to stop my destiny.

To understand their art
and know what the bible says,
as I abide in my grace-given liberty.

Everything stolen from me,
I command in the name of Jesus,
for forces of darkness
to restore back ten-fold.

I retrieve my portions…
my favor…my manifestations…
the things from God that make me whole.

O Earth,
it's time to reverse
those evil things that come my way.

They must not happen any more;
not at night nor during the day.

I renounce every strange shadow
that has overtaken my life.

I break their circle patterns,
and destroy their wicked device.

Where ever sorcery
has been practiced on me,
in the name of Jesus, I break that power too.

I renounce the soul covenant,
refusing its dominion.
I break its yoke, and every form of voodoo.

Let day and night retrieve my portions
from every witch, sorcerer, demon, evil spirit,
gangster and mafia manipulator.

In the name of Jesus,
let every spell around my life,
and every strange instrument
be broken from these evil captivators.

Let it be destroyed…every sickness…
every affliction deposited inside my life,
in Jesus' name.

Every spirit of poverty
used to surround me,
I command it back to the sender
and there to remain.

In the name of Jesus,
every spirit of ignorance,
I destroy that spirit inside and outside of me.

I break the web of blindness, distraction,
and loose my eyes to focus and to clearly see.

O God, let the altar of fellowship
between you and I be made anew.

The place of favor…the place of prayer…
the place where I commune with you.

I re-covenant my life with you, O Lord.
Heal my every wound and sore.

Remove every heavy burden
and hard yoke.
Don't allow me to reside in captivity any more!

Release me unto liberty…
the liberty of my spirit…
the liberty of my mind.

Anoint my head with new oil.
Pour into me your new wine.

Heavenly Father,
let your angels become one with me…
dwell with me…to go before
and make my crooked path straight.

Let your Spirit quicken my mortal flesh now
and begin to open my gates.

The gates of divine wealth…
the gates of anointing…
and the gates of godly devotion.

The gates of blessed feet…
the gates of abundant life…
and the gates of divine promotion."

(Jesus)…offered up prayers and supplications with strong crying and tears unto him (God) that was able to save him from death, and was heard in that he feared. Hebrews 5:7

Is any among you afflicted? let him pray. James 5:13

…in my (Jesus) name: ask, and ye shall receive, that your joy may be full. John 16:24

Chapter 3.
Overcoming Oppressive Captivity
(Using The Jesus Way CRNPF!)

One of the wisdoms involved in *Ending Abuse in Marriages and Relationships The Jesus Way* is knowing how to live among wolves. We're required to develop these survival skills because the bible says, *Let them both (the sheep and the wolves) grow together until the harvest* (Matthew 13:30). What do I do if I'm a sheep joined to a wolf? What do I do when my spirit severely suffers and grieves from the wolf's wicked attacks? How do I handle the wolves inside and outside my immediate family?

The Jesus Way **C**onfront, **R**ebuke, **N**egotiate, **P**rayer, and **F**aith (CRNPF) are God's anointed and appointed answers to the captive's questions. There are wolves, both husband and wife...both male and female...with varying degrees of sin...unsoundness of the mind... hard heartedness...and dirty hands. Some wolves will be more receptive of The Jesus Way CRNPF; whereas, others may fight against it initially, but later come in agreement. Then there are those wolves who refuse to give one inch, and because of your stand for right, will even increase their evil against you. The bible says this type individual has an anti-christ spirit; and it is from this spirit that you will need to separate...for *your* spirit's sake (John 8:24,40–47). But to those wolves who will hearken and allow themselves to feel shame and conviction, show them how to treat you by godly strategies and techniques.

If people do not CRNPF for their personal rights, the bible calls them *abusers of themselves with mankind* (I Corinthians 6:9). It goes further to say, if they are self-abusers then they're unrighteous…and if they're unrighteous then they will not inherit the kingdom of God. They have erred from the faith, and pierced themselves through with many sorrows. The bible tells us to instruct those that oppose themselves so that they can learn how to guard their spirit from grievous oppressions.

Confront–To immediately expose a trespass at the initial onset of the offense. Jesus said, *Moreover if thy brother shall trespass against thee, go and tell him his fault between thee and him alone* (Matthew 18:15). A trick of the enemy is to make you think the abuser has power over you. Confront the problem head on because you wear the helmet of salvation; and in God's order, Wisdom is better than strength. Jesus said to tell…tell…tell. *Tell* the fault one on one; and if it's refused, *tell* it to one or two witnesses; if it's still refused, *tell* it to the church (Matthew 18:15,16,17). Jesus knows that most abusers are cowards…they are great pretenders…their strength is in their concealment. When others become aware and witness the abuse, it decreases their power. If the refusal continues, know that they are more along the line of an antichrist spirit. Even though *it* is hard…and *they* are hard, you have a nutcracker…the hammer of God…His word. *"Does not my word burn like fire? asks the* LORD. *"Is it not like a mighty hammer that smashes rocks to pieces"* (Jeremiah 23:29, NLT)?

Rebuke–To immediately correct a trespass at the initial onset of the offense; a scriptural statement of defense of basic personal rights. The bible says correction is needed, lest you learn his ways and get a snare to your soul. A trick of the enemy is to make you think you're sinning if you rebuke. It's not a sin; God and Jesus are our examples in which to pattern ourselves; and they both rebuked. Jesus said, *Take heed to yourselves: If thy brother trespass against thee, rebuke him* (Luke 17:3). When Abraham wanted God to bless Ishmael, God said, *"I heard you…but my covenant will I establish with Isaac"* (Genesis 17:20–21). When out of fear Sarah lied about laughing at the idea of having a child in her old age, God rebuked her, saying, *"Nay, but thou didst laugh"* (Genesis 18:15). Jesus forced Satan's harassments to cease by rebuking him with the Word. Just as Jesus, we're to use scripture as the foundation for correction. It's okay to use sharpness in your rebuke. The bible says, Wherefore rebuke them sharply, that they may be sound in the faith (Titus 1:13). The Word of God also emphasizes that we're to use mercy when admonishing. To rebuke as brothers and sisters and not as enemies; remembering that the *true* enemy is Satan, and not flesh and blood. Another trick the enemy uses is when he tries to convince you that you're "arguing" in an effort to stop or decrease the effectiveness of the rebuke. With rebuke, you're defending your spirit; but with arguing, you're defending your flesh. A rebuke only needs to be said one time, and your spirit is content. With arguing, there is a lack of self-constraint, hastiness, and a cycle of impulsiveness. The bible says, Withhold not correction, he shall not die, and you shall deliver his soul from hell. (Proverbs 23:13–14).

Negotiate–To reach an agreement through discussion at ending injustices and violations of personal rights. God supports this technique when He tells us to come and let us reason together. Jesus instructs us to deal with injustices so that we can set boundaries for it to cease. The bible also says there comes a time for dis-annulling of commandments that cause weaknesses and is unprofitable (Hebrews 7:18). When negotiating, if you do not agree to what is being said, verbally make it a clear "No." If you fail to say "No" your silence becomes a "Yes" by default. It sets the stage for Satan to bring mischief, confusion, accusations, condemnation, and a troubled conscience. As you reach an agreement, write the established negotiations down and both parties sign. If this is left as only a verbal agreement, a trick of the enemy is for the other party to later say, "I did not say or agree to that" or "You did not say that." Always keep a copy of the signed agreement in safe-keeping for reference and confirmation. It's okay for both parties to re-negotiate as needed. Another trick of the enemy is when someone changes a negotiation in his or her mind, and fails to communicate this change or a need to return to the negotiating table to the other party. To restore order, Confront, Rebuke, and continue in the previously established negotiations or re-negotiate. It's okay to re-negotiate if that's what your spirit instructs you to do. Another trick of the enemy is to cause you to feel that you do not have the right to change your mind. Remember, if established negotiations are not working, make sound changes by following the same order: Confront that which is not working, Rebuke what is causing it not to work, and Negotiate peace for your spirit.

What do you do if negotiations or re-negotiations are refused? The scripture says, *"Do not meddle. Speak not in the ears of a fool: for he will despise the wisdom of thy words"* (Proverbs 23:9). *If any man be ignorant, let him be ignorant* (I Corinthians 14:38). *Do not give heed to commandments of men, that turn from the truth* (Titus 1:14). A strategy of the enemy is to cause you to be a peacekeeper, one who will resort to bowing, self-sacrifice and self-victimization. Jesus was a *peacemaker* and endorses us to be one, too. Deep respect can still be given without obeying a certain command that is not right. Self-negotiations can be done without your spouse's participation. Your spirit and the Holy Spirit meet together at the table and establish negotiations that are peaceable unto your spirit. Then continue the order of writing them down, sign, put a copy of them in safe-keeping, and give a copy to your spouse as well. This serves as a notice that changes will be implemented as a result of what you need for your spirit.

Prayer–To yield not to temptation and the planting and building of peace. These goals are achieved when using (Low and High) Rebuke Prayers as well as Peace Prayer. When confronted with an individual who is harassing and wants to argue, you're to initially use the (Low) Rebuke Prayer. Jesus says to *Pray that ye enter not into temptation* (Luke 22:40). Low Rebuke Prayer means to pray under your breath to the offender, saying, *"Satan, get beneath my feet. The Lord God rebukes you. The blood of Jesus prevails against you."* You're speaking this to Satan, who is a spirit; therefore, you can speak it in a low voice and Satan will hear, and not necessarily the one arguing. It is the Word that has the power and not the volume in which it's spoken. When Peter rebuked Jesus, Jesus used this technique by addressing Satan, who influenced and worked through Peter, rather than Peter himself (Matthew 16:22–23). The mightiest of God's angels, Michael, also used this technique when he contended with Satan regarding Moses' body, defeating him by simply saying, *"The Lord rebuke thee"* (Jude 1:9).

High Rebuke Prayer is used when you're being constantly harassed by an individual in his or her attempt to provoke you into an argument or fight. It is also to be used when a threat of physical harm is present. In this situation, pray loudly to the offender, for him or her to hear, saying, *"I've consulted with God! Father, forgive him (her) for he (she) knows not what he (she) does."* Satan will try to overwhelm you with multiple attacks. If an offender is not quick to cease, pray the Lord's Prayer repeatedly (Matthew 6:9–13). With this praying technique, God will shelter you in His presence, far from accusing tongues. The Lord said, *"Not by might, nor by power, but by my spirit,"* (Zechariah 4:6). And our friend, Jesus, said when we're grievously tormented, He will come and heal (Matthew 8:6–7).

God says that we do not have peace within ourselves, marriages, relationships, and the land because we do not speak it, plant it, or build upon it. Therefore peace is becoming extinct. How did Jesus speak in the bible? *Peace be unto you* (Luke 24:36). *Go in peace* (Luke 7:50). He spoke this way because our Father God also speaks in this manner...*Peace be unto thee* (Judges 6:23). We must go back to the ancient way of speaking, which is literally using the word "peace" in our daily interactions. Saying, "Good morning. Peace be unto you. Goodbye. Go in peace." When you enter your home and the homes of others, say, "Peace be unto this house." All peace that is sent out, if the person or home to which it is spoken is unworthy, it will return unto you (Matthew 10:13).

Peace Prayer is a means to establish and maintain unity in marriages and relationships. A trick of the enemy is to say there is no time for prayer. Peace prayering should be practiced daily. It is brief, but yet full of God's anointing to destroy Satan's strongholds. An example of a Marital Peace Prayer: Facing one another and holding hands, the husband prays, "God, thank you for my wife. Peace be unto you my wife." The wife prays, "God, thank you for my husband. Peace be unto you my husband." Then they together pray, "God thank you for our home. Peace be unto our home. And as for me and my house, we will serve the Lord. We go in peace." Children can be added, but first the foundation must be established between the husband and wife. King Solomon of the bible said, when the ways of people please the Lord, He makes even their enemies live at peace with them (Proverbs 16:7, NLT). And like Jesus, your home...your spirit...your peace will be restored through the power of prayer.

Faith–To fight the good fight of faith. We cannot physically fight Satan. We're commanded not to physically fight with flesh and blood (wolves) in our lives. But we're ordained and anointed to fight using our spirit's will...our faith in knowing and acting upon God's Word. We destroy Satan's devices by focusing not on the problem, but the promises of God…the blessings of Jesus Christ upon us…and the work of the Holy Spirit in our lives. These are weapons to use when fighting the fight of Faith: *the Word, Praise and Worship, Tithes and Offerings, Prayer, Fasting, Anointed Oil, Breaking Bread, and Testimonials.* More information can be acquired from a teaching poem in this chapter entitled, *The Jesus Way Training School.*

If you fail in any of the CRNPF steps; just know that Jesus already knew that you would have some setbacks while learning His way; and that's okay, He will always love you unconditionally. What displeases Him is when we refuse to ask for forgiveness, and refuse to forgive ourselves and continue in faith. Guard yourself against evil which increases to the point of physical threats and fear for your life. The bible says, *evil men and seducers shall wax worse and worse* (II Timothy 3:13). *Be not over much wickedness, neither be foolish: why should you die before your time* (Ecclesiastes 7:17)? If God releases those who freely choose to be persistent and deliberate in their sin, and turns them over to a reprobate mind; we will have to do the same. If physical violence is threatened or inflicted upon you, go to a safe haven. Ask God to direct you in your next step. Take heed to the scripture that reads, *Neither shalt thou bring an abomination into thine house, lest thou be a cursed thing like it: but thou shalt utterly detest it, and thou shalt utterly abhor it; for it is a cursed thing* (Deuteronomy 7:26). Jesus said unto the grief causing scribes and Pharisees, *For I tell you this, you will never see me again until you say, 'Bless the one who comes in the name of the Lord'* (Matthew 23:39)*!* We too are to love ourselves, protect ourselves, and preserve ourselves.

Turn and Surrender

He has him in a headlock
as he positions to stab with the knife.
The voice of his Mother rings in his head,
making him hesitate and think twice.

"Follow the ways of the Lord, my son.
This is what you do.
Don't follow after the things of the world;
the choice is left to you."

He tightens his grip around the head
as he lets the knife pierce the skin.
The voice of his Mother he begins to hear
as it invades his mind again.

"If you live by the sword, you will die by the sword.
Have compassion one for another.
The face of the Lord is against them
that do evil toward their brother."

He loosens his grip as the head wriggles free.
He drops the knife to the ground.
The intended victim scampers and breaks free,
as he hears oncoming siren sounds.

He watches him run some distances away,
as traces of blood follow too.
He thinks of his Mother and The Jesus Way,
as he mouths, "Mother, I did it for you."

"This is the police! Get your hands up!"
echoed through the quiet night.
His hands went up as he turned around,
and surrendered without a fight.

"Don't be afraid of those who want to kill you…they cannot touch your soul. Fear only God, who can destroy both soul and body in hell. Matthew 10:28, NLT

He (God) delivereth me from mine enemies: yea, thou liftest me up above those that rise up against me: thou hast delivered me from the violent man. Psalm 18:48

The Jesus Way

The Jesus Way is the path to go.
For Jesus is the Way, the Truth, and the Life,
you know?

So learn The Jesus Way.
You're defiled by
what you think, say, and do.
Displeasing to God, if defiled, are you.

To be pleasing, you must repent.
Jesus will say,
"I forgive you; now go the way I went."

Narrow is the path that leads to the Way.
Don't get off because it's narrow,
here is where you need to stay.

Leave the multitudes,
for many are not believers and disobey.
Keep the least traveled, listen to the voice of Jesus,
and do not stray.

God's Word as your lamp, and the light of Jesus up ahead,
you will not have to search for food or water,
for you'll be wonderously fed.

He that saith he abideth in him (Jesus) ought himself also so to walk, even as he walked. I John 2:6

And an highway shall be there, and a way, and it shall be called The way of holiness; the unclean shall not pass over it; but it *shall be* for those: the wayfaring men, though fools, shall not err *therein*. No lion shall be there, nor *any* ravenous beast shall go up thereon, it shall not be found there; but the redeemed shall walk *there*: Isaiah 35:8–9

Negotiation Story

Marva thought,
'It feels so nice to be out window shopping,
just to have some quiet time to myself;'
when her mobile phone rang,
and the messenger on the other end
resurfaced all the sadness earlier felt.

"Where are you?
"You need to come home now!
Why didn't you let me know
you were making another stop?"
…the barrage continues.
Marva's spirit was drained
from grieving because of threats, bullying,
and cruel innuendos.

Marva's husband, Matt, would constantly phone
telling her his every move, and wanted her,
for him, to do the same.
She felt imprisoned, suffocating,
and knew it was only through the grace of God
she had not already gone insane.

Matt always kept Marva under condemnation,
using as his weapon…her guilty conscience.
Knowing her desire is to be a good wife,
he controlled her into asking for just one more chance.

He kept her in fear with his abandoning spirit,
If she didn't follow all his rules,
he would leave.

He kept another place of dwelling
for in case she "messed up."
This kept her spirit always in a state of grieve.

Marva had confronted Matt once before
when in the bible she read,
a husband should be submissive to his wife as well.
But she quickly backed down when he puffed up,
and started to curse at her and yell.

She knew Matt would probably be gone
when she returned home,
but this time fear was surprisingly not there.
The budding joy in her spirit strengthened
and urged her on.
'If he has left,' she thought, 'I really don't care.'

When she got home, sure enough,
the house was quiet and still.
She read the usual note Matt always leave,
I'll return when you get a submissive will.

Marva knew she was at life's crossroads;
will she defend her grieving spirit or continue to betray?
She knew she had to choose whether she would please God,
or a ungodly man continue to obey.

"I always hear my Pastor say,
You cannot change what you refuse to face."
Her eyes toward God, her feet were set;
this time on a solid, even place.

The waiting game was in motion.
For weeks Matt did not call;
neither did Marva phone begging for another chance.
I'm sure Matt was wondering, 'Something's different.

It doesn't usually take this long.
Is she getting stronger over there perchance?'

Finally Matt phones asking,
"Are you fully ready to be a good wife
and do all that I say?"
"No," assuredly replied Marva.
"But I'm ready to place my life in godly order
and pattern it after The Jesus Way."

"What do you mean?"
"You talk like you done lost your mind!"
I'm not coming back! I'm gone for good!
Now you're on your own time!"

"I've been on my own time now for weeks,
and I like the way liberty feels.
It's as if you were practicing witchcraft…
grieving me and controlling my will.

You can stay where you are, if that's your choice.
See, I don't try and control your will.
I'm moving forward, even if it means without you;
for nourished and cherished
is *not* how I'm made to feel."

"What do you mean you're moving on without me?
Hold up, I'm coming home!"
It seems Matt was turning the key in the lock
before Marva had hung up the phone.

"Lets sit at the table," Marva said.
"For we have some negotiating to do."
"Okay honey, whatever you say.
I'm willing to work with you."

Turn In Your Captivity!

Marva showed Matt scriptures
that to her surprise he was willing to read.
God opened his understanding as he begins to receive:

When the righteous are in authority,
the people rejoice;
but when the wicked beareth rule,
the people moan.
God tells wicked rulers they've not obeyed Him,
but partiality in their interpretation of the law shown.

Don't threaten people. There's one lawgiver.
Who art thou that judges another?
For the Lord loves justice.
He hates wrongdoing…
controlling others to the point of smother.

Wives, don't be led astray
by nonsense from human thinking,
and evil powers of this world.
Husband, you must give honor to your wife;
she's your equal partner.
Don't show prejudice because she's a girl.

All of you are subject one to another.
This is what God has ordained.
Husbands, your authority is for edification,
not destruction, lest you should be put to shame.

Rules may seem wise, but they have no effect;
the Word of God cannot be chained.
Through wisdom is a house built,
and by understanding it's maintained.

If the husband or wife who isn't a Christian
insists on leaving, let them go.
In such cases the Christian husband or wife
is not required to stay with them, you know?

"I didn't know all this was in the bible," Matt said.
"I guess I need to take time to read.
I'm sorry I'll been so hard and controlling,
causing your spirit to grieve.

I was going by what my daddy taught me,
and what I saw as a little boy growing up.
But now it's time for God to teach me
how to cherish you with perfect love.

What do you want, honey?
What will make you smile?
Whatever you think we need to do,
we'll try that for awhile."

"To be able to come and go
in the freshness of liberty,
but show respect to you at the same time.
For me to phone
just because I want to hear your voice,
and not because I'm forced, would be divine!

To get rid of that safe house you're keeping,
which is out of godly order and disrespect to me.
For us to go to church together…
to pray together…to be joined in unity."

Matt and Marva sealed their agreed negotiations
with a family peace prayer together.
They vowed to respect, nourish and cherish
one another mutually forever.

Commit your work to the Lord, and then your plans will succeed. Proverbs 16:3, NLT

Stand your ground, putting on the sturdy belt of truth and the body armor of God's righteousness. Ephesians 6:14, NLT

By mercy and truth iniquity is purged: and by the fear of the Lord men depart from evil. Proverbs 16:6

Prove all things; hold fast that which is good.
1 Thessalonians 5:21.

In the same way, you husbands must give honor to your wives. Treat her with understanding as you live together…she is your equal partner in God's gift of new life. Peter 3:7, NLT

O God of Vengeance

Lord, the God to whom vengeance belongs!
O God of vengeance let Your glorious justice be seen!

For the evildoers gloat, voice their arrogance,
boast and are wickedly mean.

For the evildoers oppress your people, Lord,
hurting those You love.

They say, "The Lord isn't looking.
He doesn't care; this God from heaven above."

Well think again, you evildoers!
Is the One who made your ears deaf?
Is the One who formed your eyes blind?

God knows what you're doing,
and even your evil thoughts.
You'll get your punishment in due time.

The unjust claim God is on their side.
They attack the righteous,
and the innocent to death condemn.

God is a mighty rock where we can hide.
He'll make the sins of evil people
fall back upon them.

The Judge of the earth will sentence the proud
to the penalties they deserve.

God will destroy them for their sins.
For the cries of the oppressed He's heard.

God says, "At the time I have planned, I will bring justice against the wicked. Psalm 75:2, NLT

The righteous also shall see, and fear, and shall laugh at him: Psalm 52:6

Avenging Story

The Married One finally had enough,
for the Creeper had not changed his ways.

He continued to creep into the beds of other women;
refusing to hear about God,
or needing to be saved.

The Married One was just about to separate,
when the Creeper got weak and gravely ill.

He got struck with the disease of his lusts.
The disease from which many have been killed.

AIDS, the four letter word
that strikes terror in the hearts of its victims.

AIDS, the four letter word
that caused the Married One to not leave,
but stay with him.

She cared for him as best she could.
His 'other women' never came around.

"I'm sorry" could only be said with his eyes,
for with his lips, he could not make a sound.

The doctor was wonderful and gave the best care,
but nothing could stop the Creeper's demise.

Doc stood with the Married One,
lovingly holding her in support,
as the Creeper closed his eyes.

I (God) spake unto thee in thy prosperity; *but* thou saidst, I will not hear. This *hath been* thy manner from thy youth, that thou obeyedst not my voice. Jeremiah 22:21

But he shall die in the place whither they have led him captive…Jeremiah 22:12

Did You Know?

Did you know ever since people
were first placed on the earth,
the triumph of the wicked has been short lived?
Did you know ever since people
were first placed on the earth,
the joy of the ungodly is only a temporary feel?

The godless, they enjoy the taste of evilness,
letting it melt under their tongue.
They savor it, holding it long in their mouths,
refusing from their lips to let it run.

The riches they have swallowed will turn sour.
God won't let them keep it down.
Their wicked works will not be rewarded,
bringing them little joy, but many frowns.

For they oppressed…they afflicted,
and left many destitute and poor.
Their prosperity will be lost to them,
but their waste places will definitely endure.

In the midst of plenty, they will run into trouble,
and with disasters be destroyed.
God will rain down His anger,
as they try to escape,
but the arrow of God they cannot avoid.

The heavens will reveal their guilt,
and earth will testify against them hard.
This is the fate that awaits the wicked.
It's the inheritance decreed by God.

They (the wicked) are exalted for a little while, but are gone and brought low; they are taken out of the way as all *other*, and cut off as the tops of the ears of corn. Job 24:24

"On the day when I (the Lord) act…Then you will again see the difference between the righteous and the wicked, between those who serve God and those who do not." Malachi 3:17–18, NLT

Pursuit of Love

You are defined by your character…
Your Heart.
Everyone's heart has the ability
to possess the character of love.

Everyone can have it!
For it's poured
into our hearts by the Holy Spirit,
who is Love from Above.

Our hearts have the ability;
however, we will not have love,
unless we choose to pursue it.

Jesus has blessed us with
the Holy Spirit,
to assist us and help us to do it.

Only you can decide
to awaken your love,
or choose for it to remain still.

Only you can decide
to give love to others;
the most important Spiritual Law
of God's will.

For love covers a multitude of sin.
It helps us to look past offenses.

But most importantly,
it's the key to the tearing down
of captivity fences.

That's why God can command
with bold confidence
that we love our enemies and bless them.

We shouldn't say
this is something we can never do.
God is not commanding this on a whim.

Know when we would do good,
evil is present;
therefore, guard your mind
to serve the Law of God.

When your mind tries to bring you
into captivity, choose to make love
spring forth from your heart.

Just pursue the *turn in the captivity*
of your mind, and announce to Satan
you've chosen The Jesus Way.

When Satan wars against your choice,
tell him, "You're a liar!
I'm loving my enemies the way
Jesus says!"

And I (God) will give them one heart, and I will put a new spirit within you; and I will take the stony heart out of their flesh, and will give them a heart of flesh. Ezekiel 11:19

That Christ may dwell in your hearts by faith; that ye, being rooted and grounded in love, May be able to comprehend with all saints what *is* the breadth, and length, and depth, and height; And to know the love of Christ, which passeth knowledge, that ye might be filled with all the fullness of God. Ephesians 3:17–19

Beloved, if our hearts condemn us not, then have we confidence toward God. I John 3:21

...made perfect in love. I John 4:18

The Confrontation Story

Zelma finally confronted the issue
of what was making her weight increase.
She knew it stemmed from never truly feeling love
from her mother, her sister, or her niece.

She was always the one doing the *work*,
making the phone calls, and lending them money.
After praying she decided to confront them
about why they were acting so funny.

She went over to her sister's
to discuss with her how she feel.
But sister wasn't giving her much attention;
watching TV and preparing a meal.

"See that's exactly what I'm talking about,
You won't give me the time of day.
If you truly loved me,
you would listen to what I have to say."

"I'm sorry,
I guess I've taken you for granted.
You're always just so together,
while I'm always rushed and frantic.

I depend on you to keep us together.
Which, I guess, made me feel it's okay to fall apart.
I may not have been showing it,
but you're indeed truly loved in my heart."

Her niece comes in and walks right pass,
not acknowledging or saying hello.
Instead of hiding her hurt,
Zelma decided to expose it…
to let it show.

"Cherie, I need to talk with you.
I need to share some feelings
making auntie sad and blue.

You just walked right pass auntie,
not showing respect in any way.
I refuse to be treated in this offensive manner.
Next time, give me a hug and say, hey."

"Okay auntie, my bad.
I didn't mean anything by this.
I didn't know you loved to be hugged,
and wanted to receive a kiss.

You seem a little distant sometimes,
so I didn't know what to do.
But next time I'll be giving a hug
and a big ol' kiss to you."

Zelma turns beaming
with a wide smile on her face.
"Where are you going?" Her sister asks.
"I'm headed over to Mama's place."

…they devise deceitful matters against *them that are* quiet in the land. Psalm 35:20

Thou therefore gird up thy loins, and arise, and speak unto them all that I command thee: be not dismayed at their faces, lest I confound thee before them. Jeremiah 1:17

…correcting them when necessary. You have the authority to do this, so don't let anyone ignore you or disregard what you say. Titus 2:15, NLT

For God hath not given us the spirit of fear: but of power, and of love, and of a sound mind. II Timothy 1:7

Spiritual Protection

My enemies are made my footstool,
and I step on the serpent's head.
My feet are strong and mighty,
because of the daily bread I'm fed.

When my enemies came to eat up my flesh,
they stumbled and fell.
They cannot trespass against me,
no not them, nor the gates of hell.

My enemies cannot hurt me,
or harm one hair upon my head.
I can walk through the valley of the
shadow of death, and not even be scared.

There will be no prospering
of weapons formed against me.
Jesus' death and resurrection
brought me this glorious victory.

I fret not myself because of evildoers,
neither am I envious of their ways.
Any semblance of them prospering,
I know is a temporary phase.

God prepares a table before me
in the presence of my enemies.
No one can take from me what's mine,
not even those kin to me.

My steps are ordered toward power and glory.
I'm delivered from evil.
While my enemies steps are erratic,
weak and feeble.

I will fear no evil, for the Lord is with me.
I have the comfort of His rod and staff.
With the Word shining its light onto my way,
I simply walk pass the devil's wrath.

I'm redeemed from the hands of my enemies,
who cannot grab me back.
When they reach for me with outstretched hands,
their knuckles get a whack.

And they shall fight against thee; but they shall not prevail against thee; for I *am* with thee, saith the Lord, to deliver thee. Jeremiah 1:19

He shall deliver thee in six troubles: yea, in seven there shall no evil touch thee. In famine he shall redeem thee from death: and in war from the power of the sword. Thou shalt be hid from the scourge of the tongue: neither shalt thou be afraid of destruction when it cometh. At destruction and famine thou shalt laugh: neither shalt thou be afraid of the beasts of the earth. For thou shalt be in league with the stones of the field: and the beasts of the field shall be at peace with thee. And thou shalt know that thy tabernacle *shall be* in peace; and thou shalt visit thy habitation, and shalt not sin. Thou shalt know also that thy seed *shall be* great, and thine offspring as the grass of the earth. Thou shalt come to *thy* grave in a full age, like as a stock of corn cometh in his season. Job 5:19–26

For, behold, I have made thee this day a defenced city, and an iron pillar, and brazen walls against the whole land… and against the people of the land. Jeremiah 1:18

Separation Time Story

Eva's Girlfriend was still visiting at her home,
when her husband, Phil, returned, and on his usual patrol.
Drunk, and with his wickedness and meanness,
trying her peacefulness to erode.

"I thought I told you no visitors at the house?
And why didn't you answer the phone?
You probably been out with another man.
That's why I won't let you go no where alone."

"Phil, my rights will not be violated.
My environment will not be one of abuse to me.
It is written, a husband must give honor to his wife.
Dishonored and oppressed I refuse to be."

"I don't want to hit you,
but you make me do these things."
As Phil spoke, Girlfriend took a quick look
at Eva's bruised right eye,
from the previous time Phil was mean.

Eva had tried open negotiations
to address her grievances and need for change.
Phil had refused to negotiate,
instead called her crazy
and all kinds of curse names.

Normally Eva would cower in submission,
and from Phil's words flinch.
But this time when he came at her,
she stood steadfast, not moving an inch.

Sandra Wilson

In surprise, Phil thought,
Oh, she's trying to get stronger.
Just because her Girlfriend's here,
my threats don't scare her any longer?

I will make her argue
and say some really hurtful things;
then she will conform because of self-condemnation,
for speaking words that's mean.

"I told you I wanted pork chops,
but all I see is beans.
You can't cook a lick....
Your cooking's not fit for anything."

Eva knew her fight was not against Phil,
but against the kingdom of Satan.
She knew his tricks and was careful of her words
to rightfully and peacefully weigh them.

"Satan, get beneath my feet.
The Lord God rebukes you."
She continued on with,
"The blood of Jesus prevails against you too."

She said it under her breath
for Satan to hear and not particularly Phil.
She knew the power was in the Word
and not necessarily in its shrill.

"I'm not going to be pulled into an argument.
We can come to a peaceable negotiation later."
Eva was wise in not arguing,
for Phil was just trying to bait her.

She grabbed Girlfriend by the arm to follow,
leaving the area of temptation.
Phil thought, I got to say something else
that will cause her severe irritation.

"What you scared to argue?
Scared I'm a prove you wrong?
Scared I'm a make you look like a child,
as if you ain't even grown?"

"Ain't no body scared of you!" ranted Girlfriend.
"What are you doing here anyway? Phil asked.
You aint even kin!"

"Don't argue with him Girlfriend.
Let's go into the other room.
For whoever tries to fight evil with evil
is already doomed."

Phil follows them,
refusing to let peace be still.
I got to get her under my control.
I know, I'll speak of hurt and kill.

"I'll shoot both of you,
'cause I will have my way.
Remember I told you I'll kill you
if you ever start to disobey."

"She's not your child!
You can't control her will!"
"Girlfriend, come on now," Eva said.
"Let your peace be still."

Satan's use of Phil was increasing
to beyond controlling and mean.
Now he's threatening and talking about killing,
which is quite another thing.

"I've consulted with God!
Father, forgive him for he know not what he do."
This time Eva was speaking loud and open,
letting Phil know I'm praying for you.

Phil pulled a gun from his pocket,
and started waving it in the air.
Eva continued in her faith,
but this time repeating over and over
the Lord's Prayer.

"Our Father which art in heaven,
Hallowed be Thy name.
Thy Kingdom come. Thy will be done…"

Phil stood in awe thinking,
Look at this fool!
She really is breaking free
from my dominating rules!

No longer does she come running
at my beck and call.
She's become wise to the pits and snares
I've devised for her fall.

Girlfriend now was sitting quietly,
seeing the gun made her knees feeble.
Eva continued in prayer,
"And lead us not into temptation,
but deliver us from evil…"

Phil begins to feel funny.
A feeling he's never felt before.
An overwhelming feeling of,
I just can't take no more!

Turn In Your Captivity!

He bolts from the room
and heads straight out the entrance door.
Eva gives shouts of praise and glory
for God saving her life once more.

Girlfriend sighs,
"When I came over here,
I didn't know all of this was in store."
She continues to sit, but thanking God too,
for His power she could no longer ignore.

"I've stayed with Phil this long,
hoping to be the light
that convicts the change in his ways.
But now my conscience is clear," Eva said.
"Phil doesn't want to be saved.

He has an anti-christ spirit.
A reprobated mind.
God is saying I have to save myself
and separate from this kind.

God wants us wise
and not have to be saved
over and over again.
For years I've tried to be God's light,
but Phil's heart I cannot win.

I'll be leaving with you Girlfriend,
and another place of dwelling I'll find.
I'm not going to keep putting myself
in these situations. Now is my separation time."

"...the Kingdom of Heaven has been forcefully advancing, and violent people attack it." Matthew 11:12, NLT

So Jesus called them together and said, *"You know that in this world kings are tyrants and officials lord it over the people beneath them. But among you it should be quite different. Whoever wants to be a leader among you must be your servant...For even I, the Son of Man, came here not to be served but to serve others..."* Mark 10:42–45, NLT

He delivered me from my strong enemy, and from them which hated me: for they were too strong for me. Psalm 18:17

...sons have fainted, they lie at the head of all the streets... they are full of the fury of the LORD, the rebuke of thy God. Isaiah 51:20

...Because they have no changes, therefore they fear not God. Psalm 55:19

...men of corrupt minds, and destitute of the truth, supposing that gain is godliness: from such withdraw thyself. I Timothy 6:5

Turn In Your Captivity!

The Shelter Of The Most High

If you live in the shelter of the Most High,
you will find rest in the shadow of His might.
You will not fear the dangers of the day,
nor be afraid of the terrors of the night.

You can declare, "He's my God,
and I'm trusting Him for everything.
His faithfulness is my armor and protection,
sheltering me with His wings."

You will not dread the plague that stalks in darkness,
nor disaster that strikes at midday.
Though ten thousand are dying around you,
evil will not touch you in any way.

If the Lord is your refuge,
your shelter is made by the Most High.
No evil will conquer you,
no plaque to your dwelling will come nigh.

For He orders His angels
to hold you with their hands,
keeping your foot from striking a stone.
For He orders His angels
to protect you where ever you go,
if you're turned from going wrong.

You will trample down dogs and poisonous snakes.
You will crush fierce lions under your feet.
The Lord says, "I will protect those who trust in My name.
I will rescue and honor those who love Me.

Sandra Wilson

*When they call on Me, I will answer.
I AM with them in trouble and plight.
I AM the shelter of the Most High,
satisfying them with long life."*

For the oppression of the poor, for the sighing of the needy, now will I arise, saith the LORD; I will set him in safety from him that puffeth at him. Psalm 12:5

Lay not wait, O wicked man, against the dwelling of the righteous; spoil not his resting place: Proverbs 24:15

…If a man love me (Jesus), he will keep my words: and my Father will love him, and we will come unto him, and make our abode with him. John 14:23

And I will pray the Father, and he shall give you another Comforter, that he may abide with you for ever. Even the Spirit of truth; whom the world cannot receive, because it seeth him not, neither knoweth him: but ye know him; for he dwelleth with you, and shall be in you. I will not leave you comfortless: I will come to you. John 14:16–18

Fear Buster!

God has not given us the spirit of fear.
Fear is not of God.
Living under fear,
being subjected to bondage,
in your life, it should not be a part.

Fear operates under the law
of sin and death.
Jesus defeated this law on the cross.
When you accept Jesus
and choose His ways,
Spiritual Truths
now become your boss.

Be anxious for nothing,
Fear not: believe only,
and I shall be made whole.
These are Spiritual Truths,
which make you end fear and start bold.

Whatsoever ye shall bind on earth
shall be bound in heaven:
and whatsoever ye shall loose on earth
shall be loosed in heaven,
are other Spiritual Truths to incorporate.
Binding your fears
and loosening The Jesus Way
is how you change your fate.

(But remember the binding and loosening,
you have to verbally state.)

Fear reacts in anger.
Anger is a reflection of fear.
If you confront your fear,
you'll get rid of the anger;
then terror will no longer come near.

Don't accept people bondage.
A victorious lifestyle
is how you offer your life.
Refusing to operate out of fear,
will put an end to ungodly sacrifice.

Pattern your life after Spiritual Truths.
Truths are the higher rankings that be.
The fact is you may be in captivity,
but the truth is Jesus makes you free.

Whom the Lord makes free
is free indeed.
If Jesus is Lord of your life,
then you're free.
We have to learn the process
of a fear-free lifestyle…
the process of walking in liberty.

If there is pressure on you from evil,
develop the skill of fear-free.
Just declare the Word,
Spiritual Truths,
and from you the devil will flee.

So instill Spiritual Truths
down in your heart.
Force their operations down deep.
Remember them as you keep Satan
where he belongs, *under your feet*!

The fear of the Lord *is* clean…Psalm 19:9

The fear of the Lord *is* to hate evil: pride, and arrogancy, and the evil way, and the forward mouth…Proverbs 8:13

There is no fear in love; but perfect love casteth out fear; because fear hath torment. He that feareth is not made perfect in love. I John 4:18

That he (Jesus) would grant unto us, that we, being delivered out of the hand of our enemies, might serve him without fear. Luke 1:74

…we do not use words of human wisdom. We speak words given to us by the Spirit, using the Spirit's words to explain spiritual truths. But people who aren't Christians can't understand these truths from God's Spirit. It all sounds foolish to them…I Corinthians 2:13–14, NLT

The Jesus Way Training School

"Satan I'm tired of you
standing guard over my life,
as if my own life is not my matter.
Through The Jesus Way, CRNPF,
your strongholds I'm about to shatter.

Christ the Rock has okayed Himself
to be thrown through my window of fears.
I'm ready to perfect the fight of Faith,
to recover what I've missed all these years.

I've been angry at God,
deeply offended…
to where I couldn't even pray.
Offended by hurt and pain in my life
that steadfastly continued to stay.

But now I understand,
God was teaching trust in Him,
not in how I feel.
For such a time,
when I could surrender,
saying "Yes," to His perfect will.

So Satan, I announce boldly to you,
I'm joining Jesus' Training School.
I hunger to learn all The Jesus Way
skills, character and integrity rules.

I aspire to be a mighty soldier
in God's army against you.
Yes, you will be running in defeat,
after I learn exactly what to do."

"Lord, my notebook is open;
tell me what I need to know.
My gift of discern
makes me quick to learn,
as I will earnestly show."

*"I rejoice, my child,
you're no longer in ignorance and error,
but ready to show yourself approved.
I rejoice you said, "Yes,"
to The Jesus Way Training School.*

*Write down these Faith weapons
that determine how the battles
against Satan are won.
The Word, Tithes and Offerings,
Praise and Worship, Prayer, Fasting,
Anointed Oil, Breaking Bread,
and Testimonials are how you overcome.*

*You must know the Scriptures, my child;
It's your effective defense against the devil.
Study to show yourself approved
against enemies who are sly and clever.*

*The Word prevents confusion and disorder,
protecting you from being led astray.
Instilling power to say "No" to Satan,
but to Me, "Yes, I will obey."*

*All Scriptures are profitable
for correction and instruction,
helping you to avoid the gate
that leads to destruction.*

*It's your way to stop harassment,
and to resist temptation.
You're a worker for Me,
I AM the great I AM,
a higher administration.*

*It's My way of preparing you,
for what I want you to do.
It's My mighty hammer to destroy witchcraft,
sorcery, and voodoo.*

*Tithes and Offerings carry a sweet smell,
well pleasing to your Father God.
I keep the curse off you and your territory,
because to Me you did not rob.*

*Satan cannot touch you,
for I will not permit.
You can laugh at the devil, just as I,
when he throws his tantrum fits.*

*When Satan comes to do you harm,
him, I will rebuke.
You won't have room for your blessings,
when the God of Harvest gets through.*

*I prevent your fruits from being destroyed,
your harvest from lost in the field.
You'll be known as blessed,
your giving keeps you within My will.*

Praise focuses your eyes on My promises,
and not on your problems.
It refrains you from becoming offended,
for you know I'll solve them.

It reminds Satan of his former glory,
which makes him mad.
But it makes your lips joyful,
spirit arise and be glad.

Praise changes your atmosphere,
breaking evil's influence and strongholds.
It allows you to enter into My presence,
humble, but at the same time bold.

Worship means to kneel before My throne,
for I AM holy and worthy to exalt.
It protects you from Satan's condemnation,
finger pointing, and finding fault.

It allows Me to visit your body…My temple,
cleansed by Jesus' blood and name.
It helps you to surrender and obey,
in righteousness to mature and maintain.

Is any among you afflicted?
Let him pray.
The fervent prayer of the righteous
availeth much…what he say.

Prayer keeps you connected to Me…
our fellowship…requests for your needs.
When prayer is made one for another,
I bring healing because of the intercede.

*Fasting destroys Satanic yokes,
removing blinders so you can see.
It loosens bands and undo burdens,
allowing the oppressed to go free.*

*So anoint your head,
wash your face;
with a fast start to sowing.
Cause the devils who only come out
with fasting…to get to going!*

*Olive oil has the smell and taste of holiness;
I love it, to Me, it's precious.
Even the food of angels contains fresh oil;
so man should say, "Its use does truly bless us."*

*May your head never lack oil
and may it cause your face to shine.
It possesses My power…My anointing…
My glory divine!*

*Breaking of Bread strengthens your heart;
the wine makes your heart content.
It removes spiritual hunger and thirst,
helping you go the way Jesus went.*

*Eating the flesh of Jesus,
the drink of His blood,
keeps His instillment of life.
Doing this in Jesus' remembrance
is a pleasing sacrifice.*

*Breaking bread destroys
sudden fear and overwhelm;
for Satan does come like a flood.
Jesus sits upon the waters
keeping your foot from being taken.
Your confidence is restored because of His blood.*

*My Son rescues you when you honor
and bless His worth.
His glory purifies your way,
where now I can accept your works.*

*Your Testimony changes
your environmental circumstance.
It's the destruction of Satan's power,
because The Jesus Way is enhanced.*

*It keeps evil from having gainsay
over what you decree into existence.
It's faith building. So witness for Jesus!
Destroy all of Satan's resistance!*

*My cloud abides over your head,
because you're a testament and a light.
Put what you've learned into action, my child,
now you know how Satan to fight!*

Fight the good fight of faith, lay hold on eternal life, whereunto thou art also called, and hast professed a good profession before many witnesses. I Timothy 6:12

I have fought a good fight, I have finished my course, I have kept the faith: Henceforth there is laid up for me a crown of righteousness…II Timothy 4:7–8

Spiritual Warfare

Sometimes everything I do seems so hard.
I feel as if I'm always on a fight.
I'm met with opposition on every turn.
Being treated like this is not right.

The things that should be simple and easy
are met with some unusual circumstance.
I try not to get frustrated,
but is there a spiritual enemy
picking with me perchance?

I feel there's a slight torment
in my everyday activities and events.
Interacting with others
who are set on making things difficult,
is where a lot of my time is spent.

I'm glad I read the bible
and am aware of how the devil works.
He tries to steal my joy and cause defeat
by the humans he uses, called jerks.

He tries to illicit in me self-pity
and adopt the attitude, "Whoa is me."
But I'll have none of that, no self-pity here!
Because of Jesus, I have the victory!

The bible says put on the whole armor of God
so you can withstand the devil.
Yes, he will throw darts at you,
but his dart throwing won't last forever.

We all go through war and peace seasons.
There's a time for everything.
You can discern which season you're in
just as observing the signs of spring.

Jesus Christ has given us the power
to put Satan under our feet.
So stay encouraged and not intimidated
by the difficulties you meet.

We fight not against flesh and blood,
but against evil principalities.
You don't have to sin to defend yourself,
instead use your godly capabilities.

Opening your mouth and binding the devil,
will bind him in heaven too.
Remember to bind him in the name of Jesus,
and the devil will be fleeing from you.

Praising the Lord is the key
to keeping your joy inside.
The joy of the Lord is our strength,
which makes us bold and not hide.

Rejoice and be glad
you're partaking of the sufferings of Christ.
For making Jesus your choice,
and standing for what's godly right.

When the glory of Jesus Christ is revealed,
you can be glad too.
Glad you didn't allow
the stress of spiritual warfare
to get the better of you.

Then Jesus asked them, *"When I sent you out to preach the Good News and you did not have money, a traveler's bag, or extra clothing, did you lack anything?"* "No," they replied. *"But now,"* he said, *"take your money and a traveler's bag. And if you don't have a sword, sell your clothes and buy one!...* "Lord," they replied, "we have two swords among us." *"That's enough,"* he said. Luke 22:35–38, NLT

For wisdom is a defence, and money is a defence: Ecclesiastes 7:12

I am for peace: but when I speak, they are for war. Psalm 120:7

See, I have this day set thee over the nations and over the kingdoms, to root out, and to pull down, and to destroy, and to throw down, to build, and to plant. Jeremiah 1:10

For when Satan, who is completely armed, guards his palace, it is safe—-until someone who is stronger attacks and overpowers him, strips him of his weapons, and carries off his belongings. Luke 11:21, NLT

Come Out From The Inside!

We should not be as the children of Israel,
negative, complaining and refusing to persevere.

Holding to the pains of our past,
will keep us with a slave mentality fear.

With a defeated spirit,
we allow the devil to steal our destiny.

So always say to God,
"Create in me a clean heart,
and renew a right spirit within me."

We must not allow our joy to be stolen.
Thank God for what's right in your life.

We must learn to be happy,
even when things don't go our way.
For this is the sacrifice.

We must walk through the wilderness.
Walking around is not the path.

Not having the right spirit
makes our stay in the wilderness…
last and last.

Jesus has filled us with "can do" power.
Encourage yourself and "can do" power keep.

For it's better to die in faith, joy and believing,
rather than depression and defeat.

A service mentality is what we should have.
Within you, God will make His name abide.

Love and service is how you go from captive to free.
Be free so you can free others from the inside.

Don't give up, but dig in your heels
and stand your ground.

Be determined whatever your problem,
God is going to turn it around.

When life pushes you down, sit up, get up,
and set your face like a flint.

Protect your insides, by your area of weakness,
not allowing the devil a hint.

When under attack, switch your strategy
to a deeper level of consecration.

Know you can resist the devil
in your every situation.

When you've done your best
and everything you know to do, don't give up!

The problem may have you down physically,
but on your insides, in God you must trust.

We should be warriors, not whiners.
Being a cry baby and self-pity is a no-no!

Singing, praising, and attitude of faith
during adversity is what we must show.

Show the enemy you're more determined than he.
Take up your bed and walk!

Through Jesus Christ you put an end
to the devil's torment and stalk.

No emotional lying around.
No defeat, but a warrior's mind that be!

Your day of deliverance is here.
In Christ you've received the victory.

No matter how many times you get knocked down,
get back up!

God will do what He's to do,
once in Him you completely trust.

You can live and not die!
You can be strong in the Lord and His might.

By process you get stronger and stronger,
developing the skills of how to spiritually fight.

Behold, thou (God) desirest truth in the inward parts: and in the hidden *part* thou shalt make me to know wisdom.
Psalm 51:6

...*Father, into thy hands I commend my spirit*...Luke 23:46

...I (God) will put my law in their inward parts, and write it in their hearts; Jeremiah 31:33

That he would grant you...to be strengthened with might by his Spirit in the inner man. Ephesians 3:16

When Going Through

When going through the problems of life,
we must protect ourselves from depression and bitterness.
These foster self-opposition and selfish rebellion,
which only keep us in our mess.

We don't have to sink in our problems,
because we can choose to swim.
Put all your troubles under your feet,
tell Jesus you're bringing them all to Him.

If trials and tests do not come,
we're not going to grow up.
Our wilderness will follow us
until we get victory in the Law of Love.

Until we humble ourselves,
there we'll stay in our wilderness.
We must judge ourselves, surrender,
and pass all of our tests!

We're not to be angry at God
when we're going through.
To Him we're not to condemn,
contend with, instruct or reprove.

We're not to disannul God's judgment,
and try to make ourselves right.
When things don't go our way, and in our time,
we're not to fuss and fight.

For God prepares you before you receive your blessings.
Turn In Your Captivity is an appointed time.
The greater the storm; the greater the battle.
The greater the blessings will be thine.

Love, pray, bless and release them
who use and persecute you.
Ask Jesus to forgive you of your wrong,
and to purge your heart too.

Repentance unto Christ doesn't mean self-hatred.
He doesn't torment, but sends peace.
You'll say, "Ahhh, I needed that!"
Your chains of bondage will be released.

Love, pray, bless and release them.
No bitterness. Tell Satan to go away.
Command hurt and revenge to flee,
but freedom imparted to stay.

Guard against complaining and murmuring;
offer up the blood of Jesus instead.
Your yoke of bondage will remain broken,
a victorious, abundant life will be led.

There is no wisdom, nor understanding nor counsel against the Lord. Proverbs 21:30

Great peace have they which love thy (God's) law: and nothing shall offend them. Psalm 119:165

…but God had mercy on him; and not on him only, but on me also, lest I should have sorrow upon sorrow.
Philippians 2:27

The Lifter Of My Head

Yes, I get sadness that tries to linger,
but the Lord Jesus Christ
is the lifter of my head.

My happiness is restored
from the drink of life-giving waters,
and the meat of the Word
I'm fed.

Because with lies
the wicked makes my heart sad,
whom the Lord has not made sad.

Heaviness in my heart makes me stoop,
but the Lord is nigh,
lifting me, making me glad.

When my enemies try
to put my face to the ground,
the Lord touches me and sets me upright.

He puts His shield around me…
making it my glory,
confirming everything's going to be alright.

"Victory is mine!"
I can shout to the devil,
because that's what my Lord Jesus said.

Yes, my sadness dissipates,
because the Lord Jesus Christ
is the Lifter of my head.

…When the enemy shall come in like a flood, the Spirit of the Lord shall lift up a standard against him. Isaiah 59:19

But you, O Lord, are a shield around me, my glory, and the one who lifts my head high. Psalm 3:3, NLT

…he (the enemy) shall let go my captives, not for price nor reward, saith the Lord of hosts. Isaiah 45:13

Death and Confusion

Before we crossover to victory,
we have to deal with death and confusion.
This is the tearing down and clearing away
of our man-made and Satan inspired illusions.

We have to allow the dying
of whatever is binding us,
before something can be birthed.
There is a death *to* and *of* something,
before we clearly see how to put God first.

Confusion sets in
when we're about to crossover.
The enemy sends someone
to back-up our confused state.
Examine and trust in the Word,
Jesus will show you the answers,
and all your confusion will dissipate.

For every problem there's a promise.
God's promise is greater than the problem.
So go on through the process of death and confusion,
so for you, God can solve them.

...I die daily. 1 Corinthians 15:31

Who (Jesus) his own self bare our sins in his own body on the tree, that we, being dead to sins; should live unto righteousness: 1 Peter 2:24

Fear not; for thou shalt not be ashamed: neither be thou confounded; for thou shalt not be put to shame: for thou shalt forget the shame of thy youth, and shalt not remember the reproach...Isaiah 54:4

Let mine adversaries be clothed with shame, and let them cover themselves with their own confusion, as with a mantle. Psalm 109:29

"The Little Engine That Could"

I thought I could not live
without his phone calls,
or hearing his voice.

I thought I could not survive,
if being with me
was not his choice.

I thought I needed him around,
just in order to breathe.

I walked around in shock,
heart broken, wondering…
'Why did he have to leave?'

I literally had to hold my hands,
to keep from dialing the phone.

Going 24 hours
without talking to him,
was so painfully long.

Once I got through a day,
my spirit voice said, "Go for two!"

My vow to God to pass this test
is really what got me through.

As day 2 turned to 3,
my vow longed for victory.

4, 5, and 6,
my skin started to become thick.

7, 8, and 9,
I started to even challenge time.

As day 10 was achieved,
I became a little glad about his leave.

As days turned into weeks,
and weeks into months,
living time without him,
became no longer a shunt.

As a matter of fact,
I slowly gained the thought life
as the little engine tale.

You know the little engine that said,
"I think I can,"
as it struggled up the train rail.

Positive thinking and self-talk
changed it into
"The Little Engine That Could."

Same for me, I became assured,
surviving without him, I would.

I was mentally weak,
and it took The Jesus Way
to change my thought life.

Now I know the reason for his leaving
was not all me, in fact, I was a good wife.

And he (Jesus) said unto me, *My grace is sufficient for thee: for my strength is made perfect in weakness.* Most gladly therefore will I rather glory in my infirmities, that the power of Christ may rest upon me. Therefore I take pleasure in infirmities, in reproaches, in necessities, in persecutions, in distresses for Christ's sake: for when I am weak, then am I strong. II Corinthians 12:9–10

I can do all things through Christ which strengtheneth me. Philippians 4:13

…Daughter, be of good comfort; thy faith hath made thee whole. And the woman was made whole from that hour. Matthew 9:22

How Not To Be Hurt Again

I trust you, but I don't trust *in* you.

I believe you, but I don't believe *in* you.

I build my life on God's promises,
not the promises of man.
Through Christ I can do all things,
not through what man can.

When we put more value on others' opinions,
more importantly than what Jesus says;
then we lower God's shield over us,
and a people snare we raise.

We set ourselves for hurt
when we seek others for our happiness.
The hurt may be unintentional or the intent
from someone's craftiness.

Keep the shield of God up,
for letting it down exposes you.
Protect yourself from pretenders and users,
To thyself be true.

Don't put your trust *in* others,
for a people shield will fail.
Faith *in* man, rather than Jesus Christ,
brings hurt straight from the pit of hell.

Sandra Wilson

Master your emotions.
Mad and sad are feelings
the devil uses to control your life.
Refuse to excuse why you're more sensitive.
Why give the devil a self-sacrifice?

Don't sell your forgiveness:
"If you change then I'll forgive you."
Accept people owe you nothing,
not even an explanation.
Forgive by faith and choose free forgiveness
in your every situation.

If you care about your future,
refuse to disclaim it.
Believing your happiness comes from God,
open your mouth and name it.

Never let the devil see you're hurt.
Laugh when he takes his best shot.
Force others to see you're not weak,
and available for hurt, you're not.

Following the recipe on the back of the box,
can get you the cake on the front.
Mastering the skill of how not to be hurt,
makes you mature, not the runt.

You cannot have victory without a battle.
God doesn't mean for you to lose.
No man or circumstance should take your joy.
The choice is left for you to choose.

When you hurt others,
because you're hurting,
you do not understand who you are.

God desires to give you
root *in* yourself.
So choose healing for your captivity scars.

There's a difference in who you are in the world,
as opposed to whom you are in Christ.
Knowing who you are in Christ
means being complete in benefits and rights.

Some feel incomplete unless married,
if this is you, say,
"Every spiritual blessing is now in me.
I'm satisfied, perfected, assured,
confident, secured,
and people oppressed free."

Incomplete means feeling
something is wrong with you,
or you're not as smart.
Don't feel down
you're not like a particular individual.
Just use and do your part.

What you *are not*, do not matter,
if what you *are* is grounded in Christ.
Don't feel sad about not living up
to others' standards;
they may cause you torment
and ungodly sacrifice.

Your worth is not *in* what you do.
Are you worthless if you stop doing that?
Determining your value
by who you are *in* Christ,
is what makes you sound and perfect.

The love we get from the world is never enough;
always comparing, competing,
and not knowing who we are.
But the love we get from God *is* true,
unconditional and perfect love by far.

You're entitled to peace of mind and wellness.
Refuse to beg for what you're entitled to.
God's fire will make the snake come out,
and stop tormenting and harassing you.

For God is doing a new thing in you.
The new thing is in process now.
Your sowing, growth,
and fruit bearing is here.
It's okay to rejoice and say, "Wow!"

Like concrete is cracked
by a single unyielding twig,
so will you crack hurt and pain.
You have authority over your past
…forget your past hurts.
Put your trust *in* Jesus,
not a human, conditional man.

…no man stood with me, but all men forsook me…
Notwithstanding the Lord stood with me, and strengthened
me; II Timothy 4:16–17

For all flesh is as grass, and all the glory of man as the
flowers of grass. The grass withereth, and the flower thereof
falleth away. But the word of the Lord endureth for ever.
1 Peter 1:24–25

Turn In Your Captivity!

He Has Made Me Glad!

He has made me glad
I went through the pain
with just Him,
and Him alone.

He has made me glad
I went through the pain
without calling
the other on the phone.

It was my appointed time to learn
I could not use others
to take the focus away.

My pain and fears
I had to deal with myself.
It was time to stare them
squarely in the face.

It was time for me,
from myself, to stop running
and staying busy in others' lives.

It was time to deal
with my own inner torments,
and take care of my own affliction cries.

It was time for my own
self-healing, godly order,
and deliverance.

Sandra Wilson

He got my attention slowly.
It didn't burst
from a flicker
to a flame at once.

He let me know
"the wait"
and "the surrender alone"
was my trial and test.

The pain and fear
had a stronghold,
but I was determined
not to give it rest.

Through prayer
and supplication, praise,
and staying on my knees,
the chains of my captivity were broken.

(From fear and pain I was freed.)

That's why He has made me glad
I went through the pain
with just Him,
and Him alone.

That's why He has made me glad
I went through the pain
without calling
the other on the phone.

I will rejoice
for *God* has made me glad!

This was the most gratifying time
I've ever had!

Behold, we count them happy which endure…James 5:11

But let every man prove his own work, and then shall he have rejoicing in himself alone, and not in another. Galatians 6:4

Then are they glad because they be quiet; so he (God) bringeth them unto their desired haven. Psalm 107:30

He Thought

"He thought he could take my laugh away.
Ha! Ha! Ha!
He thought, to him, I would give up my life.

He thought my strength would not endure.
He thought my endurance would not suffice.

He thought his rejection of me
would cause my total defeat.

He thought his abandoning
would get me depressed
and unable to sleep.

He thought I was his captive victim,
and could never break free.

He thought I would run after him,
begging him to return
and continue to torment me.

He thought he could put dents in me,
but God made my forehead stronger than flint.

He thought forehead to forehead,
I was no competition,
but instead it was his strength that went.

His thoughts are not what mattered,
for God's thoughts are what is true.

And the same thoughts God has of me;
He has the same thoughts of you.

*For I know the thoughts that I think toward you,
saith the Lord;
thoughts of peace, and not of evil,
to give you an expected end.*

You too can walk life's journey in victory,
because on God's thoughts, not his thoughts,
are what you depend.

He thought with lies,
he could make my heart sad,
but God has not made sadness for me.

My face is strong against his face,
witnessing his defeat,
and my anticipated victory.

For though he is as a brier, thorn, and scorpion;
God commands me not to be afraid of him…
his words…nor be dismayed at his looks.

I surmise that now his thoughts are about
my power…my honor…my skill…my dominion,
the mighty woman of God he forsook."

Let this mind be in you, which was also in Christ Jesus.
Philippians 2:5

Let the wicked forsake his way, and the unrighteous man his thoughts: and let him return unto the LORD, and he will have mercy upon him; and to our God, for he will abundantly pardon. For my thoughts *are* not your thoughts, neither *are* your ways my ways, saith the LORD. Isaiah 55:7–8

Because with lies ye have made the heart of the righteous sad, whom I (God) have not made sad...Ezekiel 13:22

...therefore have I set my face like a flint, and I know that I shall not be ashamed. *He is* near that justifieth me; who will contend with me? Isaiah 50:7–8

"Thought Victor" Not "Victim"

You are a "Victor" not a "victim."
Your thinking must align
with God's purpose for your life.

Study the bible, which is God's Word,
for it makes you wise unto Satan's device.

Satan wants to have us in the victim's role,
so read the Word,
meditating on it day and night.

Through your meditation
God will reveal
when your thought life is not right.

He will impart the correct way to think,
and give you a sound mind too.

Stand on God's revelations,
because Satan will continue
to mentally mess with you.

Verbally renounce every opposing thought,
not aligned with the Word.

Repeat God's Word to Satan out loud,
and he will flee because of what he's heard.

You see the Word of God
cuts like a two-edged sword,
and causes Satan pain.

When he comes to you,
offering a messy thought life,
let the Word of God on him rain.

When you openly confess the Word,
you're changing your heart.

You're rooting out the devil's stronghold
and The Jesus Way thinking impart.

Let this mind be in you
which is also in Jesus Christ.

Guarding your thoughts
from displeasing God
is an obedient sacrifice.

So open your mouth,
using the Word of God as your fighting sword.

You'll not be confused or weak minded,
for a sound mind will be your reward.

Jesus said...*Thou shalt love the Lord thy God with all thy heart, and with all thy soul, and with all thy mind. This is the first and great commandment.* Matthew 22:37

Let them banish from their minds the very thought of doing wrong! Isaiah 55:7, NLT

For God hath not given us the spirit of fear; but of power, and of love, and of a sound mind. II Timothy 1:7

Commit thy works unto the Lord, and thy thoughts shall be established. Proverbs 16:3

"Tongue Victor" Not "Victim"

We are established as "Victors" not "victims"
by the words of our mouth.

The Word of God, not curse words,
is what we need to shout.

When things don't go our way, we should say,
"Lord, let your will be done."

When Satan tries to get us to say words of hurt,
instead his way of speaking we should shun.

Remember the bible says,
life and death is in the tongue…
words should be few and seasoned with grace.

We should not allow our words, to others,
impart a nasty, bitter taste.

If you're controlling your tongue,
you're protecting your heart.
Your heart is what God's about.

If you allow Satan to enter your heart,
then with God you forfeit clout.

Read what the bible says about controlling the tongue
and speaking the right words.

Let it be said from you,
only words of life were heard.

Whenever you speak,
remember you'll be judged
by the Law of Love.

So let your words be always pleasing to God,
Who is and Who always was.

Our tongue can bring us ruin,
destruction and shame.

It can cause us to re-enter the storm,
when out of the wilderness we just came.

The tongue is a small thing,
but what enormous damage it can do.

Ask Jesus for the skill in controlling your tongue,
and He will impart it to you.

"How long will you torture me? How long will you try to break me with your words? Ten times now you have meant to insult me. You should be ashamed of dealing with me so harshly. Job 19:1–3, NLT

Death and life *are* in the power of the tongue: and they that love it shall eat the fruit thereof. Proverbs 18:21

So speak ye...as they that shall be judged by the law of liberty. James 2:12

Sound speech, that cannot be condemned; that he that is of the contrary part my be ashamed, having no evil thing to say of you. Titus 2:8

"Action Victor" Not "Victim"

You're decreed a "Victor" not a "victim."
Your behavior plays a part in confirming this.
You must guard how you choose to act;
God doesn't want us to react amiss.

Amiss means faulty, improper, or in a wrong way.
We must conduct ourselves decently;
the way the bible says.

Once our actions create a trespass,
it will be hard to undo.
We have the grace of repentance, for sure,
but would you want these acts done to you?

Do to others
as you would have them do to you.
We must not become hypocrites,
but to our own selves remain true.

We may react wrongly out of fear.
Remember fear is the wheel Satan uses to steer.
To steer us into behaviors that displease God.
Driving us to places where our feet should not trod.

Many of us are trying to escape fears
which happened as a child, teen, or old.
If this is you, give your fears to God,
and a new creature He will mold.

Sandra Wilson

God says He will fight your battles,
so don't resist and try to do it yourself.
If you surrender, when it's your due season,
He will provide you with the help.

The help you need to win the war.
The help you requested and were waiting for.

God will bring you into His marvelous light.
It's Satan who's thrown into darkness,
blacker than night.

You're freed from captivity,
because your actions were right!
You relied upon the Lord
who taught you how to Faith fight.

For we must all appear before the judgment seat of Christ; that every one may receive the things *done* in *his* body, according to that he hath done, whether *it be* good or bad.11 Corinthians 5:10

And let us not be weary in well doing…As we have therefore opportunity, let us do good unto all *men*… Galatians 6:9–10

…when ye shall have done all those things which are commanded you, say, We are unprofitable servants: we have done that which was our duty to do. Luke 17:10

"The Wait"

Trials and difficulties in life
can make us want them over fast.

But when they linger on,
it feels like trouble will always last.

Sometimes "the wait"
is the trial we're going through.

For many of us,
God allows "the wait"
for our spirits to renew.

We must learn how to allow
Jesus to lead without a fuss.

How to will our flesh to submit,
and understand in God we trust.

"The wait" is God's way of spiritually maturing
and molding us into better.

We'll be grateful later,
when we're prepared for life's stormy weather.

We shall be as bold as a lion,
and stand as tall as an oak.

We shall better serve the Lord;
"the wait" has broken Satan's yoke.

Sandra Wilson

We shall speak words of wisdom,
and that with a sound mind.

We're victorious in every battle;
for we surrendered the "waiting" time.

I had fainted, unless I had believed to see the goodness of the Lord in the land of the living. Wait on the Lord; be of good courage, and he shall strengthen thine heart: wait, I say, on the Lord. Psalm 27:13–14

"A Time"

Just as God, over time,
delivered the Israelites out of bondage,
He will do the same for you.
Of them, you're no least.
The Lord shall fight for you,
if you just hold your peace.

You must wait God's appointed time;
as the process of grapes into a fine bottle of wine.

To every thing there is a season.
A time purposed for God's reason.

A time to be born, and a time to die.
A time to laugh, and a time to cry.

A time of war, and a time of peace.
A time to keep silent, and a time to speak.

A time to cast away, and a time to gather together.
A time to get wet, and a time to get out of the weather.

A time to rend, and a time to sew.
A time you once knew, and a time you now know.

A time to get, and a time to lose.
A time to buy new, and a time to sell used.

A time for obedience, and a time to disobey.
A time to leave, and a time to stay.

Sandra Wilson

A time to refrain, and a time to embrace.
A time to tie, and a time to unlace.

A time to mourn, and a time to dance.
A time to stand still, and a time to take a chance.

A time to breakdown, and a time to build up.
A time to be cautious, and a time to have guts.

A time to be strong, and a time to be weak.
A time to be proud, and a time to be meek.

A time to harvest, and a time to plant.
A time to rave, and a time to rant.

Why does God delay?
We couldn't handle it, if He did it any other way.

Until the time came to fulfill his word, the LORD tested… character. Psalm 105:19, NLT

…all the days of my appointed time will I wait, till my change come. Job 14:14

For yet a little while, and the wicked *shall* not *be:* yea, thou shalt diligently consider his place, and *it shall* not *be.* Psalm 37:10

…Those who are wise will find a time and a way to do what is right. Ecclesiastes 8:5, NLT

Turn In Our Captivity

A desperate, stretching reach
for the rope just within his grasp,
as the single branch he thought secure,
makes the yielding sounds he dreads.

Soaked, freezing, and tossed by the raging rapids,
he delves deep within to conjure the skills
learned in his youth, as his boat of holes
careen closer to the edge.

Sacrificing, pushing, and using
exhausted strength against the unyielding bulge,
that refuses to be evicted…
refuses to leave by the designated exit,
as she positions for the repeat.

The hushed phone call of goodbye,
the scribbled note of finality
next to the demon bottle emptied of its content,
as she staggers to bed with cramping stomach,
for her final event of sleep.

Jesus comes to our rescue and provides us
with an escape out of our tribulations,
when we think, now is the end.

Miraculous outcomes and testimonies
of the *turn in our captivities* are occurring,
because on Christ the Rock, we depend.

…Oh my Lord, if the LORD be with us, why then is all this befallen us? and where be all his miracles which our fathers told us of…And the LORD said unto him, Peace *be* unto thee; fear not: thou shalt not die. Judges 6:13,23

…Said I not unto thee, that, if thou wouldest believe, thou shouldest see the glory of God? John 11:40

Believe ye that I am able to do this? They said unto him, Yea Lord…*According to your faith be it unto you.* Matthew 9:28–29

Stand In Your Fight
The Key Is To Fight

The onslaught comes!
The fiery darts have arrived!
His wiles, to you,
the devil makes known!
The multiple attacks to rid you of
your godly assignment…
your godly favor,
Satan has devised and well sown.

Stand in your fight. The key is to fight.

Now is the time to trumpet your voice,
making the sound of travail.
Cry out the name, "JESUS!"
petitioning His help;
and about Satan's attacks begin to tell.

Resist the attacks against your voice,
fervently ask for your way of escape.
Helping and protecting angels
will be dispatched to you,
for your deliverance sake.

Stand in your fight. The key is to fight.

God also assigns people
as your helpers to victory;
so speak clearly and state
exactly the need of your request.

Sandra Wilson

Initially they may say, "No,"
but declare through them
you intend to be divinely blessed.

Maintain your integrity,
even if your request is denied,
and you're politely or rudely turned away.
Knowing they don't have the last word…
the last word is what God says.

Stand in your fight. The key is to fight

Break bread over the fight,
and watch God turn their "No" into your "Favor."
Anoint yourself,
eat the bread body,
and drink the wine blood of
our Blessed Savior.

You'll be divinely surprised,
as in Jesus you rest;
you'll receive your affirming phone call,
or your God-appointed visit of "Yes."

Stand in your fight. The key is to fight.

Even as God has turned it around,
Satan will still attempt to divert,
and even try to turn your wheel.
Just crush his fingers, elbow him off of you,
staring him in the face, say, *"No deal!"*

Speak against his wiles with your royalty authority.
Speak against being made to feel victimized.
If a tear start to swell, say, "No!"
and immediately dry your eyes.

Stand in your fight. The key is to fight.

Satan may send a cloud of confusion,
and you may do some stupid things.
Don't beat yourself up…
know that's how he works.
The smooth path Jesus had established,
off that path, you did divert.

But the fight is still on…
continue it to decree and declare…
and just keep moving.
The divert made your time a little longer
before you receive your soothing.

The fight meant for an hour
has been diverted into half a day.
But stand in your fight, the key is to fight…
from your battle do not sway.

Jesus will organize your move,
and you'll see clearly what to do.
Although you're in a strange land,
the right entrance and exit He will show to you.

Stand in your fight. The key is to fight.

Jesus said,
Don't imagine I've come to bring peace!
A man set for variance is what I've come for.
With me, I brought a sword,
and in righteousness I judge and make war.

Suppose I came to give peace?
I tell you, Nay; but rather division.
So stand in your fight. The key is to fight,
as you weld God's hammer
against Satan's head…
a Jesus appointed collision.

You'll find your way to your ordered place,
with Victory seated,
as you drive along.
He joins in with his voice of bass,
as together you shout and sing victory songs.

You're godly promoted even higher,
because you developed
the skill to spiritually fight.
Satan has checked into his hellish hospital,
because you used God's hammer
with all your might.

The way, Jesus, your friend,
taught you how to fight.

Stand in your fight. The key is to fight.

...Behold, I send my messenger before thy face, which shall prepare thy way before thee. Luke 7:27

Blessed be the LORD my strength, which teacheth my hands to war, *and* my fingers to fight: Psalm 144:1

Wherefore take unto you the whole armour of God; that ye may be able to withstand in the evil day, and having done all, to stand. Stand therefore, having your lions girt about with truth, and having on the breastplate of righteousness; And your feet shod with the preparation of the gospel of peace; Above all, taking the shield of faith, wherewith ye shall be able to quench all the fiery darts of the wicked.

And take the helmet of salvation, and the sword of the Spirit, which is the word of God. Ephesians 6:13–17

...I am set for the defense of the gospel. Philippians 1:17

Hold and Rock Me Jesus!

Hold and rock me Jesus!

Hold and rock me Lord!

Hold and rock me Jesus
with Your precious love from above!

My spirit is feeling heavy,
and fear is trying to creep back in.

My mind is under attack,
because I told Satan he wouldn't win.

I told him I have the authority
and commanded him to get beneath my feet.

I've been in spiritual warfare,
and I'm getting a little weak.

But I know where my strength comes from;
all I have to do is call Your name.

And the power of Your anointing deliverance,
strengthens and helps me sustain.

I can feel Your soothing Spirit overtake me,
as now I can no longer cry.

Your healing balm envelops me,
letting me know,
it's You who's drying my eye.

I thank You, Lord, for watching over me,
and confirming my victory is set.

All I have to do is call Your name,
and all my needs are met.

I fall down on my knees to thank You
for coming to my aid.

Total reliance upon You,
was the best step in The Jesus Way
I've made.

I love it when you,

Hold and rock me Jesus!

Hold and rock me Lord!

Hold and rock me Jesus
with Your precious love from above!

I, too, have been assigned months of futility, long and weary nights of misery. When I go to bed, I think, 'When will it be morning?' But the night drags on, and I toss till dawn. Job 7:3–4, NLT

And he (God) saw that *there was* no man, and wondered that *there was* no intercessor; therefore his arm brought salvation…and his righteouness, it sustained…Isaiah 59:16

As one whom his mother comforteth, so will I comfort you, and ye shall be comforted...Isaiah 66:13

...praise God our savior! For each day he carries us in his arms. Psalm 68:19, NLT

...God my Creator, the one who gives songs in the night? Job 35:10, NLT

The Call

I was at the drive-through menu at Burger King,
when my name rung out.
I thought it may be a friend, which of me had seen,
as I inquisitively begin to look about.

I thought a friend's face I would find at the car,
only to be startled to find no one near or seen afar.

I felt it was of God, but I wasn't sure.
Would God give such a wonderful sign
on this journey of mine to walk pure?

To clear my confusion,
again came the call,
deep within the spirit realm as I slept.
My eyes opened with the realization
of the majesty of His voice…
a voice so unusual…I wept.

As if in a flood of many waters,
my name was spoken, *S-AND-RA*.
I praised God,
for this encouragement was the best,
on my Jesus Way journey so far.

God really sees me!
He really knows what's going on
in the lives of the ones He call!
Now I'm attentive to the hearing of His voice
where ever I go…to the gym…to the bank…
and even to the mall.

Sandra Wilson

The voice of the Lord *is* upon the waters: the God of glory thundereth: the Lord *is* upon many waters. The voice of the Lord *is* powerful; the voice of the Lord *is* full of majesty. Psalm 29:3–4

…Fear not: for I have redeemed thee, I have called *thee* by thy name: thou *art* mine. Isaiah 43:1

A Feather On The Couch

I found a feather on the couch,
and my inner voice spoke,
"This is from God."

I pondered the meaning of the feather.
Yes, I pondered it kinda hard.

Then my spirit said,
"Go get the bible,
the answer there I'm sure you'll find."

To my divine surprise,
the image on the front of the bible
looked just like the feather of mine!

It was the New Living Translation Bible,
and the image was a combination
of a feather and the sun.

It was a sign from God
rewarding me for the deeper walk
of surrenderance I'd begun.

God was confirming
that He was with me,
in my *new life* free from being oppressed.

This too was a precious and divine sign
from God, I must confess.

Sandra Wilson

I sang praises and thanked Him, for to me,
the feather was like a ram in the bush.

I laughed to myself as I conversed with God, saying,
"Who knew the couch would be for more
than just placing my tush?"

I am weary with my groaning; all the night make I my bed to swim; I water my couch with my tears. Psalm 6:6

…If now I have found grace in thy sight, then shew me a sign that thou talkest with me. Judges 6:17

God's Mighty Hammer!

The burning throbbed and traveled down,
as I attempted to soothe the wasp sting away.
This was the second sting to my head this week.
These wasps were mean and didn't play.

They were unusually aggressive,
as they stood guard at my entrance door.
Of my twenty-two years at this home,
I've never had this problem before.

Earlier God had given me in a dream,
to use His hammer to smash witchcraft's head.
Puzzled and inquiring about the hammer,
God directed me to this scripture that read:

"Does not my word burn like fire?"
asks the Lord. *"Is it not like a mighty hammer*
that smashes rocks to pieces?"
Why were these wasps only stinging me,
and had not even bothered my nieces?

I had been standing on God's revelation,
using His mighty hammer
against every captivity in my life.
Now these wasps were attacking my head,
trying to get me to run in fright.

But I'm not running from you Satan!
All your tactics will not prevail!
I'm going to keep using God's mighty hammer,
and send *you* running straight back to hell!

Sandra Wilson

"Does not my word burn like fire?" asks the Lord. "Is it not like a mighty hammer that smashes rocks to pieces?" Jeremiah 23:29

I have wounded them that they were not able to rise: they are fallen under my feet. Psalm 18:38

That thy foot may be dipped in the blood of *thine* enemies, *and* the tongue of thy dogs in the same. Psalm 68:23

Again, God's Mighty Hammer!

The mighty hammer of God
smashes rocks to pieces.
It does the same to Satan,
who causes cruelties and hurt.

Hold God's hammer
in your right hand,
and start to smashing.
Watch the pieces of Satanic rocks
fall to the dirt.

The rocks in your life
appeared massive and impenetrable.
You wondered how will it ever
be brought down?

When you didn't know
about the hammer,
and was using something else,
not a chip or dent in the rocks
could be found.

But praise be to God!
He made you aware,
His hammer,
you're appointed to use.

Hold the hammer up high
and bring it down hard.
Allow it on the head
of Satan to bruise.

Smash down Satan's strongholds!
Break his back!
Illicit another blow!

Keep smashing until Satanic
influence and witchcraft crumble.
You have God's legal authority
to use His hammer, you know?

Lying beneath your feet
in defeated pieces is Satan,
so don't lay the hammer down
or store it away.

The name and blood of Jesus,
with God's mighty hammer,
are the supreme weapons
to force evil to obey.

God's mighty hammer
is His Word, His covenant.
He said it,
so it must come to pass.

Keep using God's hammer
and you will grow
from strength to strength;
power to power;
glory to glory;
and everlasting to ever last.

Who but our God is a solid rock? Psalm 18:31, NLT

Come to Christ, who is the living cornerstone of God's temple...And now God is building you, as living stones, into his spiritual temple. 1 Peter 2:4–5, NLT

But they refused to hearken...Yea, they made their hearts *as* an admanant stone...Zechariah 7:11–12

They threw me into a pit and dropped stones on me. Lamentations 3:53, NLT

...thou (Lord) hast subdued under me those that rose up against me. Psalm 18:39

And ye shall tread down the wicked; for they shall be ashes under the soles of your feet...Malachi 4:3

Then did I beat them small as the dust before the wind: I did cast them out as dirt in the streets. Psalm 18:42

Like Bees

Though the thoughts swarmed
like bees around my head,
I dismissed them as lies.
I was now aware of Satan's devices,
and of his many tries.

He can no longer sting me,
for his stinger has been pulled away.
I refuse to be chased around.
The path to Jesus is where I stay.

With boldness I take back the honey.
Yes, the honey promised to me.
For the beehive is within my reach,
and the climb is easy up the tree.

I can hear the sound of the buzzing around,
but I'm not afraid of Satan's device.
For my beekeeper's protective wear
was given to me,
by my friend, Jesus Christ.

They (evildoers) compassed me about; yea, they compassed me about: but in the name of the LORD I will destroy them. They encompassed me about like bees; they are quenched as the fire of thorns: for in the name of the LORD I will destroy them. Thou hast thrust sore at me that I might fall: but the Lord helped me. Psalm 118:11–13

…for God hath scattered the bones of him that encampeth *against* thee: Psalm 53:5

…Righteousness covered me like a robe, and I wore justice like a turban. Job 29:14, NLT

…honeycomb, sweet to the soul, and health to the bones. Proverbs 16:24

The Growl

The audible sound of growling,
as of a mad, vicious dog,
reached my ears.
I hastened to my car that was parked,
as I managed to control my fears.

What was making that sound?
Was there a dog after me?
I turned in the direction of the sound,
only to find nothing to see.

The growling came from a dark corner
on the side of my home.
There was nothing there but darkness,
but yet I felt I wasn't alone.

Something was mad and did not want
what was happening to me.
I was breaking the poverty stronghold
off my family tree.

I had blessed my niece with my old car,
in order to enrich her life.
God had blessed me with this new car,
to seal the victory in my spiritual fight.

Evil comes out at night,
snarling like vicious dogs
as they prowl the streets.
Just as the Lord laughs at them,
I laugh too at their defeat.

To the dealership was my direction,
to finalize the deal.
The growling did nothing but confirm
I was in God's will.

Watch out for those dogs, those wicked men and their evil deeds…Philippians 3:2, NLT

They return at evening: they make a noise like a dog, and go round about the city. Behold, they belch out with their mouth: swords *are* in their lips: for who, *say they*, doth hear? Psalm 59:6–7

Give not that which is holy unto the dogs…lest they trample them under their feet, and turn again and rend you. Matthew 7:6

…No one's family or inheritance is safe with you around! But this is what the Lord says: "I will reward your evil with evil; you won't be able to escape! After I am through with you, none of you will ever again walk proudly in the streets." Micah 2:2–3, NLT

The Repo Man

I had been paying for a van
I didn't have,
for more than three years.

My abandoning husband
had run off with it;
but my godly obedience
not to try to get it back,
continued to subdue my fears.

All during those years,
I was financially blessed
to keep my head above water.

When my funds would get low,
God gave me favor,
confirming He was my Heavenly Father.

Through it all,
I was spiritually maturing
and learning The Jesus Way.

The Holy Spirit's guidance
was so satisfying,
until it was easy for me to obey.

The pride of the abandoner
made him think,
"I'm safely out of town.
No one, from me, can take the van away."

God allowed him a season of prospering,
space to repent…
but he didn't.
Now comes my season of repay.

God released me from my vow,
no longer will I pay for *him*…
no longer will *he* have the van.

God took care of that
through the use of His evil angel…
the evil angel called the repo man.

God forced my hand,
I was released to confront.
I had been victorious
in my obedience and wait.

Information I gave to the repo man,
to help him, the van take.

Although the abandoner knew he was coming,
he could not outsmart God's plan.

Although he knew he was coming,
The van still became the possession
of the repo man.

(Taking the van from my husband
was just the start of God's plan.
Now He had to help *me* get the van
from the repo man.)

In honor of my release,
I had named it The Jesus Van.

In honor of its name,
God took it from the repo man.

The payment deadline,
in order to retrieve,
was just one more day.

I had come to accept
it was just repossessed,
because the amount of money
I could not pay.

Now I know
how Abraham must have felt
…his ram in the bush…
way of escape he did not miss.

Because I know
how I felt,
God blessed me with the money
from my loving and blessed Sis.

The abandoner phoned, stating,
he would give my divorce,
and remove his name from my house.

I hung up,
praising the Hand of God.
For the abandoner sounded as humbled
as a little ol' church mouse.

But that's not the end
of the van story.
God spoke it was my double release
into someone else's life.

It was released unto the one
who spoke a double blessing over me,
also freeing her from her captive plight.

Turn In Your Captivity!

Victory in The Jesus Way!
Not by giving evil for evil…
plotting…competing…retaliating…
and evil kill.

Victory in The Jesus Way!
By blessing my enemy…
obeying…waiting…enduring…
and staying within God's will.

Human plans, no matter how wise or well advised, cannot stand against the Lord. Proverbs 21:30, NLT

And Jesus replied, *"I assure you that everyone who has given up…property, for my sake and for the Good News, will receive now in return, a hundred times over…property—-with persecutions. And in the world to come they will have eternal life…"* Mark 10:29–30, NLT

For your shame *ye shall have* double; and *for* confusion they shall rejoice in their portion: therefore in their land they shall possess the double: everlasting joy shall be unto them. Isaiah 61:7

Chapter 4.
Living in Victory
(The Jesus Way!)

These anointed poems have aided in your achieving from God the *Turn In Your Captivity, and the end to abuse in your marriage and relationships through The Jesus Way.* Your enemy's season of reign is over, and now you can enjoy the fruits of your Jesus Way labor. Evil and wickedness have been captured and placed in chains and put into a pit of iron. For the Word says, those who lead in captivity, shall go into captivity (Revelation 13:10). You have learned to invade Satan's palace, overpower him, strip him of his weapons, and carry off the spoils… rewards…promises…and all that had been stolen from you. Satan and his team have been rooted out, pulled down, destroyed, and thrown into outer darkness, bounded by hands and feet, and bleeding from their crushed heads. In place of their evicted space is personal peace and joy, along with unity in marriages and relationships. He who held you captive and tormented in an imprisoned home has now received godly correction and godly order. For those who had to release and separate from an anti-christ spirit, God has stabilized you with abundant life and manifested promises.

In marriages both husband and wife receive care from one another equally as God has ordained. Daily "Peace Prayer" has brought much needed closeness, fellowship, honor and respect to one another. Negotiations and re-negotiations were effective in establishing peaceful stability; therefore, Confront and Rebuke are rarely needed. There are still on occasions disagreements; but now you and your spouse disagree without being disagreeable.

There is a season of rest and reaping from your earlier season of spiritual warfare. Now your peace extends to your children and other relationships: family, friends, co-workers, and even your enemies. There is healing of past wounds and old offences. Living under the Law of Love allowed you to receive the promises of God. You have the same joy that was also in Christ Jesus. Poems of love and reconciliation have replaced hurt and pain.

The Jesus Way has assisted you in your transition from an oppressed life to an established life of resurrection, restoration, and rewards. Ashes have been swept away by beauty; mourning has been quieted by oils of joy; and the spirit of heaviness has been torn away in exchange for a garment of praise.

Whoever Is Victorious

Whoever is victorious
will not be hurt by the second death.

They will eat from the tree of life
in the paradise of God's wealth.

Whoever is victorious
will eat of the manna
that has been hidden away.

And each one
will be given a white stone
engraved with their new name,
only for their display.

Whoever is victorious
and obey to the end,
will be given authority
and receive the morning star.

Whoever is victorious
will be clothed in white…
white that's without any blemish,
spot or mar.

They'll never have their names erased,
for in the Book of Life,
their names, they'll find.

And Jesus will announce
before His Father and angels,
"Those names in the Book,
they're Mine."

Whoever is victorious
will become pillars in the Temple of God,
and will never have to leave.

And the new names
Jesus inscribes upon them…
those new names will eternally cleave.

New Jerusalem
will come down from heaven,
and citizens in that city, they'll be.

And everyone will be invited
to sit with Jesus on His throne.
Yes, everyone who's deemed victoriously.

God will give those victorious a harp,
so the song of Moses
and the song of the Lamb they can sing.

They will receive an invitation
to the wedding feast of the Lamb,
the Son of God, the King of kings.

…The labourer is worthy of his reward. I Timothy 5:18

You Thrill Me Lord!

You thrill me Lord!
I sing for joy because of what You have done!
You allowed the godly to flourish like palm trees
and grow strong like the cedars of Lebanon!

Although the wicked may flourish like weeds,
and evildoers blossom with success,
only eternal destruction is ahead of them.
But You are exalted in the heavens, O Lord.
Your enemies will surely perish…
evildoers…scattered and condemned.

You have made me as strong as a wild bull.
How refreshed I am by Your powers that be!
With my own ears, I've heard
the defeat of my wicked opponents.
With my own eyes, I've seen
the downfall of my enemies.

Even in old age, the godly will still produce fruit.
They will remain vital and green.
They will declare, "The Lord is just! He's my rock!
There's nothing but goodness in Him I've seen!"

Happy are those who fear the Lord. Yes, happy are those who delight in doing what he commands. Their children will be successful everywhere; an entire generation of godly people will be blessed. They themselves will be wealthy, and their godly deeds will never be forgotten. When darkness overtakes the godly, light will come burning in. They are generous, compassionate, and righteous. All goes well for those who are generous, who lend freely and conduct their business fairly. Such people will not be overcome by evil circumstances. Those who are righteous will be long remembered. They do not fear bad news; they confidently trust the Lord to care for them. They are confident and fearless and can face their foes triumphantly. Psalms 112:1–8, NLT

What A Wonderful Time!

"What a wonderful time!

What a wonderful day!

What a wonderful time
to be in The Jesus Way!"

Thy Word, O Lord,
is settled in heaven!

Let the earth rejoice
and say,

"What a wonderful time!

What a wonderful day!

What a wonderful time
to be in The Jesus Way!"

The *turn in your captivity*
is now complete!

So shout for joy,
and emphatically say,

"What a wonderful time!

What a wonderful day!

What a wonderful time
to be in The Jesus Way!"

The statues of the L\ord *are* right, rejoicing the heart...
Psalm 19:8

Publish his glorious deeds among the nations. Tell everyone about the amazing things he does. Psalm 96:3, NLT

My Man

You're my Protector, Provider, Partner,
and my godly Man.

You work long hours for me and the children.
You're always doing the best you can.

Your eagle eye sees what needs to be done,
and you do it with skill and ease.

You're sweet and do special things for me,
because for me, you're willing to please.

You do not lead with an iron clad fist,
but you direct as the loving hand of God.

That type of king I can follow.
That style of leadership is smart.

You have the fear of God,
and direct your family with His ways in mind.

Our daily Peace Prayer
has caused our love to endure,
and stand against the test of time.

So I applaud you for your character, my Love,
and our children give you a hand.

You're my Protector, Provider, Partner,
and my godly Man.

For the husband is the head of the wife, even as Christ is the head of the church: and he is the saviour of the body. Ephesians 5:23

Nevertheless let every one of you (husbands) in particular so love his wife even as himself; and the wife *see* that she reverence *her* husband. Ephesians 5:33

...their first responsibility is to show godliness at home...This is something that pleases God very much. I Timothy 5:4, NLT

On The Wings Of Love

When you said the words, "I love you,"
as you looked tenderly into my face.
I told myself to stay calm,
but my heart had a faster pace.

What started as a jog,
picked up a sprinter's speed.
It got faster as I heard you ask,
"Will you please marry me?"

I felt my feet lift off the ground
as wings sprouted and I took flight.
With your love I felt I could fly even higher,
as I flapped with all my might.

My spirit continued its elevation
till the stars were within my touch.
I soared pass the stars into the brilliant galaxy,
because I never felt loved so much.

I tried to hold my emotions back,
but they flooded right through my gates.
The gate of 'Love Is Forever'
and the gate of 'I Can't Wait.'

I can't wait to start my life
with someone as special as you.
I can't wait to say the eternal words of love,
"I Do."

A word fitly spoken *is like* apples of gold in pictures of silver. Proverbs 25:11

...I am ready to come to you; and I will not be burdensome to you: for I seek not yours, but you...II Corinthians 12:14

Reminds Me Of Our Love

The gentle spring breeze
dancing lightly upon my face.
Reminds me of our love.

The sweet and fresh smell
after an April shower day.
Reminds me of our love.

A warm sock just plucked
from the dryer's heat.
Reminds me of our love.

Soft and cuddly slippers
upon my feet.
Reminds me of our love.

Two whales swimming the ocean,
side by side.
Reminds me of our love.

Sea shells left from the receding tide.
Reminds me of our love.

All these reminders contribute to
the appreciation of our love.

Having you in my life is a blessing,
given to me from Who is and Who always was.

So let the reminders keep coming,
and the awesomeness of our love grow.
I will keep loving you more each day,
and continue my appreciation to show.

I thank my God upon every remembrance of you. Philippians 1:3

…they will be encouraged and knit together by strong ties of love. Colossians 2:2, NLT

2 (Two)

2 peas in a pod,
describes our love.

2 kites soaring high
upon the breeze,
with strings intertwined.

2 soft cuddly slippers
placed at a warm winter's fire.

2 plates arranged
for a romantic dinner,
with wine.

2 gether for ever,
we will always be!

2 day and every day
our love makes history!

That there should be no schism in the body; but that the members should have the same care one for another.
1 Corinthians 12:25

And I will give them one heart…Ezekiel 11:19

…so then they are no more twain, but one flesh. Mark 10:8

For there is a man whose labour *is* in wisdom, and in knowledge, and in equity; Ecclesiastes 2:21

…the Lord…with righteousness shall he judge the world, and the people with equality. Psalm 98:9

Your Smile

Your smile captures my heart
and speaks to me in so many ways.

It tells of a friendship blossomed into love.
A love that makes us both unafraid.

Unafraid to reveal our true feelings
and lay our weaknesses on the line.

Unafraid to cling to each other,
knowing our love will grow
even stronger with time.

So keep on smiling,
and showing those beautiful pearly whites.

For to you I give my heart,
and I give it without fright.

But I rejoiced in the Lord greatly, that now at the last your care of me hath flourished again; wherein ye were also careful…Philippians 4:10

And having this confidence, I know that I shall abide and continue with you…Philippians 1:25

…So love truth and peace. Zechariah 8:19, NLT

A merry heart maketh a cheerful countenance: Proverbs 15:13

Sweet Music Together

My Love, we make sweet music together.
Our music has a beat and a rhythm that exist.
We sway in unison to its rhythm,
and its beat we never miss.

We combine our focus to the notes on our scale.
Our Love is made even sweeter,
by the high notes we held.

Blues, Country, R&B, or any sheet music you find,
we have no difficulty in singing it,
because our Love is musically inclined.

So let the drummer boy, tap,
and the rapper singer, rap;
our music is what will last forever.

Let's sing our Love Song as loud as we can,
because we make sweet music together.

Thy watchmen shall lift up the voice; with the voice together shall they sing: for they shall see eye to eye... Isaiah 52:8

...Love is what binds us all together in perfect harmony. Colossians 3:14, NLT

...admonishing one another in psalms and hymns and spiritual songs, singing with grace in your hearts to the Lord. Colossians 3:16

Then thou shalt see, and flow together...Isaiah 60:5

Forgive Me

Forgive me for the fight
we had.
I know you're probably still
seeing red.

I wish I could take back
what I did to you,
and the awful words I said.

Just know my actions
came out of fear emotions,
and not out of my heart.

I will always love you,
and in my life
you're an integral part.

So turn that red into a color of white,
and tell me you love me too.

So I can grab your hand
and never let go,
as we walk the love path anew.

BUT I determined this with myself, that I would not come

again to you in heaviness. For if I make you sorry, who is he then that maketh me glad, but the same which is made sorry by me?…not that ye should be grieved, but that ye might know the love which I have more abundantly unto you. II Corinthians 2:1–2, 4

Be humble and gentle. Be patient with each other, making allowance for each other's faults because of your love. Ephesians 4:2, NLT

Always keep yourselves united in the Holy Spirit, and bind yourselves together with peace. Ephesians 4:3, NLT

Still A Sister Of Mine

The winds of rivalry
may have come between us at one time,
but you're still a sister of mine.

The things we said
and did have no reason or rhyme,
but you're still a sister of mine.

Let's put our differences aside,
so we can remain a family together.

If rivalry shows its winds again,
we can command it to leave forever.

You're still, and always will,
throughout the tests of time,
be a sister of mine.

And all things *are* of God, who hath reconciled us to himself by Jesus Christ, and hath given to us the ministry of reconciliation…God was in Christ, reconciling the world unto himself, not imputing their trespasses unto them; and hath committed unto us the word of reconciliation. Now then we are ambassadors for Christ…II Corinthians 5:18–20

...that thou observe these things without preferring one before another, doing nothing by partiality. 1 Timothy 5:21

Therefore if thou bring thy gift to the altar, and there rememberest that thy brother (sister) hath ought against thee; Leave there thy gift before the altar, and go thy way; first be reconciled to thy brother (sister), and then come and offer thy gift. Matthew 5:23–24

Brother

My sweet dear brother
I love you a ton!

You run errands for me
I don't have time to run.

You fix things around my house
I'd been meaning too.

And not a penny you charge
after your carpentry work is through.

You drive me places
so I don't drive alone.

You give me brotherly advice,
and you never steer me wrong.

There are so many sweet,
dear things you do.

I thank God for blessing me
with a brother like you!

…a brother is born for adversity. Proverbs 17:17

Young men likewise exhort to be sober minded. In all things shewing thyself a pattern of good works: In doctrine *shewing* uncorruptness, gravity, sincerity, Sound speech, that cannot be condemned; that he that is of the contrary part may be ashamed, having no evil thing to say of you. Titus 2:6–8

LET brotherly love continue. Hebrews 13:1

Daddy

Thank you Daddy for guiding me
on how to be a success in life.

Your counsel still burns within me,
gaining victory over problems without strife.

Your words of wisdom and revelations
seep into my very being.

You open my eyes to many a things
I'm blind from seeing.

I thank you for my nurturing
from the wells of my heart.

Success in life, I can grab it, it's free,
from what in me you impart!

And he (God) shall turn the heart of the fathers to the children, and the heart of the children to their fathers... Malachi 4:6

...be blameless, the husband of one wife, having faithful children not accused of riot or unruly. For a bishop must be blameless, as the steward of God; not self willed, not soon angry, not given to wine, no striker, not given to filthy lucre; But a lover of hospitality, a lover of good men, sober, just, holy, temperate; Holding fast the faithful word as he hath been taught that he may be able by sound doctrine both to exhort and to convince the gainsayers...That the aged men be sober, grave, temperate, sound in faith, in charity, in patience. Titus 1:6–9; 2:2

"Mama, Thank You"

I thank you Mama for loving me
and showing me life's way.

For making me, "Get up!"
when in bed I wanted to stay.

For inspiring in me
that my goals I can achieve…
and achieve them well.

For picking me up
and brushing me off,
whenever I hit a road block and fell.

For being my biggest fan,
and my cheerleader too.

There are no words
to sum it up, but simply,
"Mama, thank you!"

The aged women…that *they be* in behaviour as becometh holiness, not false accusers, not given to much wine, teachers of good things; That they may teach the young women to be sober, to love their husbands, to love their children, To be discreet, chaste, keepers at home, good, obedient to their own husbands, that the word of God be not blasphemed.
Titus 2:3–5

Well reported of for good works; if she have brought up children, if she have lodged strangers, if she have washed the saints' feet, if she have relieved the afflicted, if she have diligently followed every good work. 1 Timothy 5:10

Thy mother is like a vine in thy blood planted by the waters: Ezekiel 19:10

My Mama's Dedication

Mama, your children truly miss you.
We think about your loving smile
and your quiet way.
Those memories will carry us through
many a difficult day.

The gentle way you would say, "Yeah,"
when asked, "Mama, are you alright?"
The smile you would give us as you awoke
and caught us watching over you
through the night.

Our childhood years of a Mama,
young, strong and tall.
Our teenage years of a Mama,
as determined as a brick wall.

Our older years of a Mama,
whose time was winding down.
Our years today of a Mama,
who we had to place in the ground.

But that is not the end of years,
there is still an event to come.
When my Mama will awake to a sound,
but not the sound of a fired gun.

With the sound of a trumpet,
the dead in Christ shall arise.
They will be caught up to meet Him
in the heavenly skies.

I can envision my Mama arising
with that same gentle smile.
But my Mama has changed,
as they say, by a country mile.

No longer is she quiet and still,
but really quite loud.
She is praising Christ the King,
as she disappears beyond the cloud.

For the Lord himself shall descend from heaven with a shout, with the voice of the archangel, and with the trump of God: and the dead in Christ shall rise first. Then we which are alive *and* remain shall be caught up together with them in the clouds, to meet the Lord in the air: and so shall we ever be with the Lord. 1 Thessalonians 4:16–17

My Family Love Memories

"Hey here! Ya'll come on in!"
was the voice of my Grandmama,
as she elicited a hug only a Grandmama could give,
...and imparted into my soul such peace!

"Whoopee!"
was the sound she would sigh,
as the stress of the day she would release.

"Don't step on the back of my shoe no mo'!"
was the command my Grandmama would make.

And the look she would give,
"What am I gonna do with this child?"
as once again I made that dreaded mistake.

Once my Grandmama broke a hog's nose
with a piece of stove wood.
She didn't play!

Whatever she told you...
that one time,
was all she had to say.

There was nothing my Grandmama couldn't do.
She worked hard all her life.

It brings tears to my eyes as I think about
all she sacrificed.

She was gentle and loving,
but firm and strong, at the same time.

And how she could cook on that wood burning stove!
There's only one word to sum it up…
"Divine!"

"Now ya'll eat til ya'll get enough,"
was the statement of love my Granddaddy would make,
finishing first at the table and preparing to leave.

He was a great provider and showed his love,
by making sure his family's appetites were appeased.

I learned as a child,
you had to be careful around Granddaddy,
or a spit of snuff,
you would find on your clothes.

It was your responsibility to outsmart the spit.
Because what direction the snuff would go…
only Granddaddy knowed.

A brief visit to the city,
was all Granddaddy would endure.
"DaDa, please stay. You just got here."
"No! Take me home. I'm ready to go!"

Granddaddy would stay in the city,
about an hour,
…and not too much mo.'

Like my Grandmama,
he was strong-willed,
and his love for things of the country was iron-clad.

He was a quiet, gentle and peaceable man,
but if you tried to stop DaDa from plowing in the field,
now that's what could get him really mad.

"Quit Fred!"
are the words I awaked to most mornings,
as cousins Stanley and Fred played tussle
in Grandmama's kitchen.

Shushing each other to be quiet
before Grandmama came
and start to switching.

A jokester, cousin Stanley was,
loving to laugh and play.

As a family,
we wouldn't have had it any other way.

"Put Grandmama's hot plate down!
Look Fred, she's always trying to fix her hair."

A memory I recall with fondness,
as Stanley positioned himself to poke fun…
and to stare.

Just like Grandmama,
uncle Bus could tell stories
that would make your hair stand on end.

So descriptive…he made it so real,
you didn't even have to pretend.

While walking down the road to go fishing,
uncle Bus said a haint asked him,
"Where you 'gwine?"

By the time he finished the story,
we were laughing so hard;
we're actually crying.

Uncle Johnny Jr. was a jokester too.

He had his special way of showing
his love for you.

As a young child,
and explaining to Grandmama
why I had peed in the bed,
uncle Johnny Jr., laughing at my alibi,
blew my cover.

But he made it up to me,
by creating me to be a chocolate milk lover.

I awaited his return from school,
because from his lunch he would save.

On his return home,
his carton of chocolate milk,
…to me he gave.

Cousin Linda Kaye, what an angel!
On this earth lived!

She kept a smile and a sweet spirit,
even when she was ill.

She loved to talk girlie talk,
and when she would giggle,
to her mouth went her hand.

To me,
she had the heart of Jesus,
and was a long-suffering, godly wo-man.

Aunt Betty was the queen of jokes.
She always saw the funny side,
and caused you to see it too.

And if you were a fat-jawed baby,
aunt Betty was gonna bite you!

She loved to have fun with words,
like calling thighs…"yams,"
and talking about…"the booty."

This was her way of loving;
revealing her inner beauty.

Aunt Betty's famous line about marriage:
"Its not all booty and face."

She may have been laughing when she spoke it,
but it's wisdom that can't be replaced.

Aunt Betty had an eye for decorating,
and she loved nice things.
That's why I know she's in heaven,
with a spectacular pair of wings!

We had another jokester in the family, uncle L.T.
His heart was one I would characterize as
…being free.

When I was a young girl,
uncle L.T. would laugh,
saying my daddy wore 'a boot and a shoe.'

My sister and I would exclaim,
"No he don't!"
Because talking about our daddy,
was something no one was allowed to do!

Turn In Your Captivity!

As we cried and protested,
trying to convince him to take it back,
his laughter grew even louder.

As I think about this memory
of uncle L.T....
my heart grows even prouder.

Taris, my second cousin,
I didn't get to know him well.

But he sure could dance and rap,
are the memories others tell.

To me he appeared a quiet young man,
full of fun and love.

More memories will be made with Taris,
when we join him in heaven above.

Cousin Marilyn knew what she loved,
and bugs were not it.

If a bug got on cousin Marilyn,
she would have a downright fit.

She was very particular,
but with her family, she loved free.

With her re-dedicated life to God,
cousin Marilyn got the victory!

Marvin, my brother,
he was smart and always one step ahead.

We could never beat him to the cornflakes.
He was always at the table, smiling,
already well fed.

He was serious about his food,
and his family too.

Where ever Marvin saw the need,
he was always willing to do.

He's a solider in heaven now,
as he was on earth.

He's loving his Heavenly Father
with the same love given,
the earthly father of his birth.

What a writer and an awesome woman,
my mama, Annie Bell was!
Ya'll just don't know!

In the early morning,
Annie Bell would write,
and from her the words would flow.

She could also draw.
A cartoonist was more her style.

These are the types of things
to Annie Bell's face would bring a smile.

She loved her family.
We were her life,
and she unselfishly gave to us.

My mama just kept that gentle,
soft smile, and never made a fuss.

To all the families of the earth,
with relatives gone on ahead.

We, the Washington and Bryson family,
celebrate with you the life your relatives led.

We all have memories of our family,
we cherish in our hearts.

May we all have beautiful family reunions,
so lots more memories can start.

…that without ceasing I have remembrance of thee in my prayers night and day; Greatly desiring to see thee… II Timothy 1:3–4

But I would not have you to be ignorant, brethren, concerning them which are asleep, that ye sorrow not, even as others which have no hope. For if we believe that Jesus died and rose again, even so them also which sleep in Jesus will God bring with him. I Thessalonians 4:13–14

And he (God) said unto me, It is done. Revelation 21:6

*For he spake, and it was done; he commanded,
and it stood fast. Psalm* 33:9

Bibliography

The poem, *Morning Glory*, is a collaborative inspiration from the book, *Meditations For Women Who Do Too Much*, copyright © 1990 by Anne Wilson

Schaef/HarperCollins Publishers Inc.; and the song, *Maybe She's Just A Morning Glory*, Track 10, by Liz Wright from her music CD, Salt.

Data regarding Intimate Partner Abuse (IPV) from Wellesley Centers for Women, Wellesley College, 106 Central Street, Wellesley, MA 02481 USA

Turn In Your Captivity, Ending Abuse in Marriages and Relationships The Jesus Way will be beneficial to:

Outreach Ministries

Women and Men Conferences

Mental Health Facilities

Abuse Shelters

The Prison Systems

Weight Loss/Eating Disorder Programs

Marriage Counseling Programs

Single's Ministry
Teen Counseling Programs
Substance Abuse Programs

For correspondence or to book **Sandra Wilson** as a speaker:

Log on to the website at: www.sandrawilson.net and/or www.thejesuswaysite.com